Hunger for Life

A Memoir

Candace Heather

Published by third.hill

Print Edition © December 2016

ISBN: 9781520294612

Version: 2017-01-01

The Twelve Steps are reprinted with the permission of Alcoholics Anonymous World Services, Inc. Permission to reprint and adapt the Twelve Steps does not mean that A.A. is in any way affiliated with this program. A.A. is a program of recovery from alcoholism only- use of the Steps in connection with programs and activities which are patterned after A.A., but which address other addictions, does not imply otherwise.

Every reasonable effort has been made to contact relevant rights owners of material included in part III of this book. Such persons are invited to contact us.

Cover layout design © third.hill, cover illustration license purchased from iStockphoto.com

Nothing in this book should be taken as medical advice or diagnosis, and you should always consult with a qualified medical practitioner before starting any health programme or if you have any concerns about your health. The author does not accept any responsibility for any loss or harm that may occur from your use or misuse of this book or your failure to seek appropriate medical advice.

Dedication

To Simon and my beloved P and D. To the other heroes in my life: my parents, sister and brothers.

To KS, MD and MA.

Acknowledgements

Deep gratitude to my mother, sister and cousin for reading, proof-reading and commenting on the manuscript in its many forms. Grateful thanks to Kay Sheppard for her permission to quote and refer to her literature and for her on-going support.

Author's Note
The stories in this book are true. In an effort to safeguard
the privacy of certain individuals, some of the names of the
people mentioned have been changed

Contents

Introduction

In 1986 when I discovered the first label I could attach to my illness, there were only a few books on bulimia nervosa (literally, appetite of an ox). They described the symptoms, the extreme behaviours and the suffering of the affected people and their families. No one really knew how to treat it then and (in terms of orthodox medicine in the UK) very few offer effective and long-term treatment methods today. Health professionals are only just beginning to accept the one vital component that has been overlooked, misunderstood or denied for so long: that bulimia is actually a manifestation of food addiction and that food addiction is as real as alcoholism or heroin addiction.

Outside of standard orthodox treatment, there's now a range of effective programmes for recovery from food addiction, which includes bulimia and Binge Eating Disorder. The most successful involve following a food plan which avoids all binge trigger foods and combines various 'tools' to enable the sufferer to learn to cope with emotions and negative thought patterns rather than resorting to food, drink or drugs to blot out their feelings. These two components— abstaining from the substance and working a programme— are the bedrock of many addiction recovery programmes. I'm most familiar with Kay Sheppard's programme of recovery which includes fully comprehensive literature, research-based information into the biogenetic nature of the disease, case studies and an effective and practical food plan and programme for living in recovery. (Visit kaysheppard.com to learn more and see also other resources in Chapter 32).

The book is divided into three parts: the first part covers my experience of growing up with disordered eating and my search for a solution together with the encounters I had with various practitioners. The second part covers 23 years of psychological slavery to a cult-like therapist—a practitioner who undoubtedly saved my life but went on to keep me and many other women as emotional and psychological hostages; forcing us to sever contact with our families and even children. The third section discusses the disease of food addiction, a healthy food plan and recovery programme together with a selection of the various psychological tools that have finally enabled me to live a life beyond my wildest dreams.

Though the second part is at times harrowing, disturbing and downright bizarre and will be totally incomprehensible to all but those who are desperate for recovery, it may help to bring attention to those practitioners who abuse their positions of power.

What I'm ultimately trying to achieve by writing about my experiences is to raise awareness of a workable solution for sufferers, their families and anyone who wants to help those who have reached desperation point and are willing to do whatever it takes to recover. After all, there are only three paths for those of us who are food addicts, or indeed addicts of any type: recovery, insanity or death. Death from suicide is only too common amongst people with eating disorders. The lives of far too many girls and women (although not exclusively a disease for females) are being lost this way.

Part I

Chapter 1: Wednesday's Child

For some reason I always hated what I looked like. I don't know whether I was genetically predisposed to being vain or whether I just didn't live up to the exaggerated appearance of my Barbie dolls with their huge heads, masses of blond hair, tiny waists and long legs. Perhaps I simply bought into the age-old obsession that beauty is the most important quality in a woman. Perhaps it was living in a value system that overlooks emotional health as being as critical as physical health. Either way, I was obsessed with my weight, what I looked like and how I came across from a very early age.

I remember defacing photos of myself and turning my framed school photo around and drawing a witch on it instead. I remember changing my clothes numerous times throughout the day but never feeling right about how I looked. I didn't like my nearly black hair, turned up nose and dark hazel eyes and particularly hated my eyebrows which I was certain were conspiring to meet in the middle.

My concerns about my appearance were extreme even as a toddler. I remember an incident on a camping holiday in Brittany where my siblings and I were at the beach with my father waiting for my mother to join us with our swimming costumes. My father wanted us to play in our underwear until she arrived but knowing my knickers were old and tattered, I was desperate to avoid being seen in them. So while my father was absorbed in making a car out of sand for my brother, I sneaked off to follow the narrow winding path that led up through the cliffs to the campsite, expecting to meet my mother coming in the opposite direction.

As I approached the top I was distracted for a moment by a small brown lizard running across my path. Interest in the creature soon turned to panic as I suddenly realised that there was no sign of my mother and I had no idea where I was. With my desperately deficient sense of direction (which is just as bad today) I ended up wandering around a supermarket until a mother with two small children of her own took me under her wing. My father, on finding me after a frantic search, thanked her politely and walked me calmly back to our tent for a hiding. I never wandered off again.

Back at home, not long after our holiday, a large wart appeared in the area under my nose and above my lip. I very soon earned the nickname Warthog. It was affectionately applied by my parents and siblings but I felt miserable and hated the name and hated the wart. I was booked in to hospital for it to be removed and remember screaming at the top of my lungs as something sharp went in to my backside. The last thing I remember before the anaesthetic took effect was the acrid smell that hit my nostrils as a gauze swab was applied to my upper lip. The wart gone, I soon lost the nickname.

* * *

I suppose my background would be considered fairly privileged and middle class. I was the third of four children with an older sister and brother and a younger brother who came along six years after me. We lived in large comfortable homes with bannisters to slide down and lots of space to play and rooms to hide in. Although my father believed in being very strict, he loved us dearly.

Growing up in the 60s and 70s, we had a very traditional upbringing. My father was a patent and trademark agent and would leave in the morning carrying his briefcase and wearing a pinstripe suit, white starched shirt, waistcoat and a bowler hat. My mother stayed at home with us until we started school and I remember the fun I had as I helped her around the house. I loved it when she made the beds on top of me while I lay on them and remember the soft fabric of the sheets falling gently onto the soles of my feet. The highlight of the week, however, was a trip to the launderette—*The Bon Temps* as it was euphemistically called. I would stand mesmerised at the front of the enormous tumble dryers, keeping track of a favourite dress or top. Best of all was watching my mother feed the damp sheets through the huge rollers to iron them as billows of steam would hide her small frame each time.

For just over a year my cousins came to live with us which meant that my mother cared for five children, all but one under school age. My auntie had called in one day to ask my mother to look after my cousins while she went shopping but never returned. It was the last time any of us set eyes on her.

There were many fights between my older brother and me over the years but plenty of times of closeness and hysterical laughter too—particularly the games we invented in the car on long journeys. One pretty disgusting game had us shrieking with laughter as we'd stick pieces of spit-moistened tissue up our nostrils and snort them out at each other. There were no seatbelts in the backs of cars in those days and we'd lie on our backs, clutching our knees to our chests and roll around in the boot of our old Saab estate; eagerly waiting for the next time the car turned a corner.

I loved and looked up to my sister who was three years older than me, although I always felt she was the good daughter and I was the bad one. When babysitters were in short supply we would go with my parents to their friends' homes in our nighties and sleep in their double beds while the grown-ups were all having dinner. My sister would pretend she'd suddenly been possessed by the spirit of a witch and I played along as I enjoyed being half scared and half amused at her performances. I found out recently that she'd worried for ages that she'd traumatised me as a result. When my younger brother arrived, I adored him—we all did. He was the most wonderful mistake my parents ever made.

In addition to my obsession over my appearance, I also seemed to have been dealt a disproportionate share of anxiety and fear as well as a strong tendency to feel and take responsibility for other people's pain. When I was a young child in kindergarten, one of the rare, lovely teachers, Miss Davidson, would sing a song to us that would break my heart and have me in floods of tears every time:

I left my baby lying there, lying there, a-lying there.
I left my baby lying there to go and gather blaeberries
Hovan, hovan gorry ogo I lost my darling baby oh.[1]

I felt my parents' pain acutely. My mother had had a particularly sad start to her life. Her father had died of TB when she was five and she'd been sent to a boarding school from about the same age. She had suffered bullying from the older girls which ranged from having her knickers taken down and being forced to sit among the stinging nettles in the playing fields to being dangled by the ankles over the bannisters above the stairwell on the top floor.

I remember watching my mother trying to swim underwater one day, frantically flailing her arms and feet around, bottom in the air, trying to submerge. She looked so vulnerable I wanted to cry. Hearing a story where my dad was left on his own as a child at a rained-off boy-scout outing with a soggy bag of sandwiches and a bottle of 'pop' was equally painful. These memories stayed with me throughout my childhood.

I worried constantly over the safety of my parents too. Whenever they'd been out and were due to come home I would sit by the window waiting, willing and praying for them to come home, imagining car crashes or accidents that would mean I'd never see them again. If they were very late back, I would be on the brink of tears and then feel a surge of relief as their car pulled up into the drive.

And then there was the fear. My sleep was filled with nightmares and I would awaken terrified from a bad dream in need of comfort from my mother. It wasn't an easy task to get to her though. The first hurdle was my older brother. If he woke up he would send me back to my room and I'd have to go back and wait until he fell asleep again. But if I managed to get past his bedroom, the next leg of the journey was even harder. Holding my breath for fear of waking my father, I would plan every step to avoid the floorboards that creaked. When I finally made it to my parents' bedroom, I would go on all fours and crawl slowly to my mother's side of the bed, curl up on the floor and go to sleep. Sometimes she would wake up and pull me into bed next to her. It was sheer bliss as I snuggled into her arms and forgot my dream.

Other times the cold would wake me up and I would creep back to my bedroom—one agonising step after the other—but comforted enough to have been near her.

I had a recurring nightmare throughout my early childhood of a man's face that would appear in front of me as if suspended in the darkness of my room. He spoke only on one occasion in my dreams, 'YOU WILL NEVER ESCAPE ME.' It was the most terrifying of all the versions of the nightmare as I dreamt there was a howling gale in my room, tearing at my bed covers as I clung on to them with all my strength. The next morning I found myself huddled in the corner of my bedroom, bed clothes strewn across the floor. Night terrors had no name in those days.

Another night-time fear that scared the wits out of me was a kind of sleep paralysis where I would be conscious but unable to move. It was desperately frightening and I would try to force myself out of it. Eventually, I would be able to wiggle a toe or a finger, then a related limb and finally a sudden, gasping return to full functionality. What made it all the more frightening was that often the fear of sleep paralysis was enough to bring on an episode.

As I grew older, the nightmares were replaced by a number of pet fears that took turns in dominating my imagination. They ranged from fear of my parents' death; fear of a polystyrene wig stand in the attic that was made to look like Anne Boleyn's severed head (a prop for a school play, complete with bloody neck); fear of being buried alive;

rabies (fuelled by the 'La Rage' posters routinely posted on Ferries at the time); the water shortage (1976); plague (courtesy of a television drama called 'The Survivors'); and nuclear war.

I was tormented by these fears and I don't know why I didn't tell my parents. When I did eventually mention rabies to my father he said, 'I won't let any nasty dogs get you'. That was all it took; the fear left completely in an instant and never returned.

When my parents were ill on two particular occasions I remember praying non-stop for their recovery, believing that if I stopped it would be the finish of them. My father had pneumonia and was ill for some time though far from death's door. My mother was in bed for a few days with a kidney infection but again it wasn't life-threatening. My sister said the doctor had looked very serious when examining her but I interpreted that as meaning she was dying.

While she was ill, I had to leave for a children's camp and on the first night I shared my fears with a girl who was in the same tent as me. It was a bad idea. She told me she'd seen the face of death before her mum had actually died. Almost as soon as she said it, a scene started to unfold in my mind. A man's head, covered in mud and blood with the whites of his eyes shining, began to emerge from a shallow grave. It filled me with absolute terror the entire time and I was convinced my mother would be gone by the time I got home. She was fine of course.

Outside of the comforts of home and family I was painfully shy and self-conscious and used to look down at the ground with my jaw jutting out rather than make eye-contact with people. I always assumed everyone was talking about me behind my back and was told I often walked around looking anguished and full of self-pity. I remember my mother buying me a poster to go on my bedroom wall; it was an ostrich with its beak wide open looking alarmed. The caption read 'I take everything personally!' I didn't understand it at the time but looking back now I can clearly see why.

Despite the love of my family, having best friends in and outside school and a cousin that was more like a sister, I always felt like an outsider; that I never fitted in.

Chapter 2: Anaesthesia

From an early age my relationship with food seemed to be abnormal and together with my acute self-consciousness and constant feelings of anxiety made for a miserable time at school. I was convinced that my teachers despised me and all but a few seemed to delight in their sarcasm and disparaging remarks. Having VICTIM 'stamped' on my face with my anguished expression made me easy prey. Mealtimes were a source of extreme anxiety both from the perspective of the food itself and the school policy to insist on pupils eating everything on their plate.

At lunch time, we would put on our overalls and file downstairs to the basement for our meals. The dining rooms were in the old dormitories as the school had once boarded pupils. The rooms were dark, hot and claustrophobic.

As with many young children I was a fussy eater but I think my gag reflex was particularly sensitive. I have a very keen sense of smell too (an inherited trait from my mother) which may be why I had such extreme reactions to food. It was love or hate.

The smell that reached my nostrils usually gave me an indication of what we were having for lunch and I would start to heave after descending only a few steps into the basement. Cauliflower cheese, cheese flan with whole plum tomatoes ladled on top, macaroni cheese and burgers would set my stomach churning. All but a few meals were so over processed they were unrecognisable. The school burgers were particularly foul; I don't know what they did to them but the only similar taste I've ever experienced was when my mother heated up some canned burgers on a camping holiday one year—even my father couldn't eat them.

Presiding over mealtimes and first aid was Matron. Eagle-eyed, frightening and a bully, she would say grace and we'd be reminded to sit in absolute silence throughout our meal. She would wave her large serving spoon over the dumb waiter to signal the kitchen staff to hoist up the food for each course. It was meant to be a joke but had worn rather thin from daily use. I would frantically hope for something nice for lunch given that every scrap had to be polished off and we were constantly reminded of the starving children in Ethiopia.

Everyone struggled with vegetables, especially Brussels sprouts which were always cooked to death and resembled yellow slime. It was the combination of texture and smell that made me gag and, to make matters worse, our food was always cold by the time we sat down at the table. As soon as the lids were lifted on the serving dishes and the scent of over-cooked cabbage, sprouts or swede intensified, I would get that watery feeling in my mouth that precedes vomiting.

I couldn't bear some of the puddings too; Rum Baba, stewed green plums with custard and Gypsy Tart were the most offensive and sickening to me. Many of us would conceal food in the pockets of our overalls, but a whole meal obviously couldn't fit in. When canned tomatoes were on the menu I was in trouble as they would create very obvious red, soggy bulges in my pockets. On one occasion Matron forced me to turn out my pockets and eat the contents; some of which was several days old. My sister clearly remembers Matron making her eat mouldy peas from her pocket a few years before me and she still can't stomach them today.

I was always the last one in the dining room and often ended up being force-fed. On one occasion I was trying to eat a mound of cold plum tomatoes one tiny morsel at a time, swallowing each piece with water. The tomatoes languished on my plate skinless and anaemic as Matron came over to me, held my head, pinched my nose and started to force-feed me. She put her other hand over my mouth until I swallowed. I coughed and heaved and when she shovelled the last mouthful in, my body rebelled and I projectile-vomited tomatoes and cheese flan all over her and the table.

Matron dragged me by my hair and clothes up to see Miss Jenner, the headmistress, who was even more frightening than Matron. I stood in front of her in her office while she loomed over me in her black cape. She bawled at me and I wet myself in fear; warm pee filling my shoes and overflowing onto her oriental rug. I must have been about five at the time.

But when it was minced beef pie followed by syrup and sponge, I was in rapture. I hardly noticed my friends at the table, I was transported away by the taste of the food and Matron didn't have to pin me down or send me to sit outside for talking. I went straight up for 'seconds' as soon as I'd finished. For a short while afterwards I was high and I felt wonderful. The world was okay and I would mess about making my friends laugh.

At home my mother's food was healthy, plentiful and delicious. She made the best roast dinners in the world: fluffy and crisped roast potatoes, Paxo stuffing with vegetables that were cooked to perfection. The only thing I couldn't stand was bubble-and-squeak but we didn't have it very often. I remember retching as I tried to eat yesterday's fried up cabbage. In my anger at the bubble-and-squeak, I smeared a Dairylea cheese triangle over the glass panels in the lounge door and earned a sore backside as a result.

At mealtimes, we would sit and wait for our dinner with hands in our laps and elbows off the table under threat of a rap across the knuckles with the carving fork.

'How much is this costing us, Daphne?' my father would groan and add, half-teasing, 'Bread and jam is good enough for them'.

Even though I felt full after dinner I was never satisfied and wanted more. I was neither aware that I was comfort eating nor conscious that I was gradually becoming completely numb to my feelings. At some level, then, I learned that food worked very well as an anaesthetic and it stopped me feeling anyone else's pain too.

At the end of the school day I would feel very down and just wanted to eat from the moment I walked out of the gates until I went to bed. I would tell my mother how the girls would say mean things to me and she would always reply, 'They're just jealous, ignore them'.

From the teachers I got black mark after black mark which led to a detention most nights. Three black marks meant one detention. I can't really remember why I got so many; although I know I talked too much in class and wore my outdoor shoes indoors and vice versa.

After school I would buy crisps from the sweet shop next door and when we got home I would steal from the kitchen cupboards. At first it was just the jelly cubes from the larder that I took as they were at a level I could reach and I also remember taking a tin of syrup which I kept hidden in my bedroom. When I was tall enough to reach the bread and cereal cupboards by climbing on a chair, I stole more and more. Every night when I came home from school I would eat snacks until dinner time then continue to eat cornflakes loaded with sugar; salad cream sandwiches; peanuts and choc ices throughout the evening. I would sit in the stairwell of our upstairs lounge with my head poking up into the room trying to conceal how much I was eating from my siblings. I would go up and down the stairs which led to the kitchen via a passageway that was once the old pantry and would load up with snacks on each visit. I loved toast and would climb on to a chair to reach the grill and cook several slices at once; often too impatient to wait for both sides to cook.

My parents worked hard and, it being the 70s, played hard too. As a result they were usually out in the evenings either at choir practice or at friends' houses for bridge and dinner. Or they'd be in the dining room entertaining friends at home. My mother also enjoyed performing in or directing plays at the local drama group and would often be out at rehearsals while my father played squash. This worked to my advantage and I was able to take food without being seen on most occasions. Our baby sitters were usually more engrossed in their boyfriends or the television to wonder where I kept disappearing to.

Once, when I was refuelling on a night my parents were entertaining at home, I heard voices and hid in the larder. Unfortunately that was where my father was heading as he wanted to show off the office den he'd built which could only be accessed through the larder. I was dragged out, frantically trying to chew and swallow a mouthful of cooking chocolate. To make matters worse I was only wearing a jumper and a pair of knickers at the time so I felt greedy, fat and ashamed.

All the extra food I was consuming had the expected effect and by the time I was 12 I hated my body. I despised the rolls of fat on my stomach that appeared when I sat down and would cross my arms in front of my stomach trying to conceal the spare tyre that protruded from under the waistband of my pale blue school tunic. I wasn't huge but was definitely chubby—what people used to call puppy fat. When a relative saw me in my unflattering puffed-sleeved leotard with tight elasticated leg holes and remarked on my bulging thighs—I became desperate to do something about it.

At around the same time I overheard a conversation at school where one of the girls said 'God, Candace is ugly!' and it cut to the core. I had a pudding-basin haircut which I hated. It was supposed to look like Joanna Lumley's at the time (a 'Purdy' haircut after her character in the TV series The Avengers) but our hairdresser had a fairly small repertoire. At camp, a friend said to me out of the blue 'God, you're ugly!' and although she said it with a laugh I believed her as I had just seen my school photos with my gone-wrong Purdy hairstyle and hated them. It was time to take action.

.

Chapter 3: Dying to Lose

I asked my mother to buy me some slimming sweets, known as Ayds, which were supposed to suppress my appetite but they just made me want to eat more. I then tried Dr Richard Mackarness's 'Eat Fat Grow Slim' diet that had worked for my mother. It was the predecessor to the Atkins diet but based on exactly the same principles of eating high protein and fat foods and restricting carbohydrates. I lived on tins of sterilised cream, bacon, eggs, cheeses of all types and avoided bread, fruit and vegetables. I lost weight quickly and was very pleased with how I looked. I felt I looked more grown up and feminine compared to the chunky tom-boy I looked like before. I also started to shape my eyebrows and wear make-up and was amazed at the difference eyeliner and mascara made to my face. I felt pretty for the first time in my life.

At school I was suddenly able to focus on my school-work outside the fog of sugar-induced hangovers. I was moved up from 'bottom group maths' to 'top group maths'. My friends noticed a change in my personality as well—I was no longer the class clown and impressionist, instead I was seen as a boring goody-goody. In fact two close friends started to call me Cuboid to reinforce how square they thought I'd become.

By the time I was 14 I was slim but not excessively so. However, my parents were concerned and took me to see our GP. He confirmed I was a reasonable weight and handed me a calorie-counting sheet. I remember sticking it in the bin and thinking it was a waste of time as I was avoiding carbs rather than counting calories.

Not long after this I discovered diabetic sweets and chocolate. The label claimed they were sugar free but they were actually loaded with another type of sugar, known as sorbitol. I started to insist on my mother stopping at the local chemist on the way home from school every day so I could run in and buy some. They caused terrible diarrhoea and painful stomach cramps and although the pain was horrible I felt lighter and thinner afterwards and so I began to associate them with weight loss.

I found a copy of a book on anorexia that my mum had on her bedside table at the time and clearly remember the image on the front of a mangled knife and fork. At some level, finding the book made me feel special as I assumed my mother thought anorexia might be an issue for me. It discussed the various extreme measures that people used to try to prevent the absorption of calories. I learned about laxatives, diuretics and other drugs. Of course with laxatives they don't actually make you lose weight but the fluid loss registers on the scales and so I believed they were a quick way of avoiding weight gain. This was my 'how-to' guide to practicing bulimia. I had no idea that what I was doing was dangerous and I thought I'd found a way of eating what I wanted without having to endure the consequences.

By this time I was even more obsessed with my appearance. I remember dancing in front of my wardrobe mirror in a mini skirt with high heels and was completely transfixed by my now slim legs. I lived for the weekend where I could show off my new clothes at our youth club and would stare awkwardly at the boys, afraid to talk to them but wanting them to notice me.

I remember shopping in the High Street on one occasion and buying some anti-cellulite cream and some ExLax. The dosage on the laxative packet stated one small chunk but I ate the whole bar. In the morning when I went downstairs to the toilet I passed out and smashed my head on the corner of the radiator. I came to in a pool of blood on the bathroom floor and went down to tell my mother. I was as white as a sheet when I walked into the kitchen and it must have looked like I'd poured theatrical blood over myself. My mother, my sister and I had all experienced episodic bouts of fainting so no one suspected that I had suffered anything but an innocent blackout. My head was badly cut though so I was taken to hospital.

I didn't know it at the time but later discovered that ExLax contains a substance called Phenolphthalein which, if taken to excess, can cause a drop in blood pressure, dizziness and collapse. I was taken to hospital where I had my head stitched up and was admitted to a children's ward for a couple of days to observe the concussion. While I was there the doctors carried out several tests to try to find out why I had fainted. I didn't tell anyone that I had taken laxatives. To me, taking too many laxatives was shameful and embarrassing; I didn't even consider the possible effects on my health.

One doctor said I had an irregular heartbeat when he listened to my chest. I discovered later that another effect of laxative abuse is the disturbance of electrolytes which can cause arrhythmias. I didn't take much notice at the time as I was mortified by the fact that he was listening to my bare chest with my immature breasts on display topped with disproportionately large nipples which I detested. His cheeks were flushed red and I assumed he was embarrassed at the sight of them.

I remained at a weight I was happy with until I was about 16. My O' Level results were fairly good: French, German and English literature were my favourite subjects although I enjoyed maths and biology too. To study for my A levels I sat and passed the entrance exam for my brother's school which had started to allow girls to join the sixth form. In the end, however, I decided to follow my sister to go to the local grammar school she'd attended. I liked the idea of going to school locally and of saving my father the fees of either my brother's school or my current school.

As for my diet, I gradually started to include carbohydrates, pasta and bread at mealtimes and my weight started to go up as a result. By about 17 after my boyfriend said to me, 'Nice legs, bit large though' I decided to go on a calorie controlled diet with a friend at school and we both started a regime of trying to stick to 600 calories a day. This time I lost a dramatic amount of weight and I was on a high. I loved looking at my skinny arms and the gap between my thighs; I loved my protruding hip bones and my skinny fingers.

My boyfriend at the time was at Manchester University and I would go up to visit him at the weekend. All I could think of was how I looked and what he would think as I arrived in my tiny pink pedal pushers and pink stiletto slingbacks. I lived for going to nightclubs and showing off and the rest of the time I was starving myself and taking laxatives.

I don't remember making a conscious decision not to take ExLax again but the experience of ending up in hospital must have registered at some level. Instead I took stimulant laxatives (usually containing senna) which act on the colon to pass food through it more quickly. Multiply the single tablet dosage by 50 and the effect on the colon muscle is horrific. But I soon found out that any laxative could cause me to pass out and I simply thought it was the pain that caused me to faint. Little did I know that at any time I could have collapsed and died.

In the evenings the laxatives would kick in and I would spend ages in pub or nightclub toilets with queues of angry women waiting for me to vacate the loo. Back at my boyfriend's filthy student house-share in Moss Side, I would rush to the outside toilet and curl into a ball on the ground in excruciating pain from the stomach cramps. I would stare up at the various fungi sprouting around the loo until I would either drag myself back onto the toilet or black out on the floor. I was surviving on a ridiculously low calorific intake and stayed this way for just over a year.

The time came, however, when I suddenly flipped from starving myself from day to day to losing complete control of my eating and bingeing in a way I'd never done before. I started to increase the laxative use and a few days of starvation would be punctuated by bingeing and purging in between. This signified the end of my 'anorexic' phase and happened while I was at a wedding with my boyfriend and his family. I had decided I would eat just one roll for lunch but something in me snapped and I kept going up for more and more, hiding what I was eating so no one was aware. I bought some laxatives and took the whole bottle.

Later that evening when we went home by train, the 100 laxative tablets took their toll. I was nauseous and my hands started to get pins and needles and I knew I was going to black out. My hands went numb and I rushed for the toilet. Nothing but sheer agony can describe the pain of laxative abuse. I slumped on the floor of the dirty toilet, soaked with other people's urine and sodden toilet paper, alternatively throwing up and sitting on the toilet. Though I told myself 'never again' I knew that I had crossed the line and there would be no going back to controlled eating.

I hated purging—detested it and I was scared and angry at having this awful disease. But I was desperate not to put on weight and, to me, purging was the only solution. A friend at school had gone through a skinny phase and then suddenly ballooned. I was frantic that I wouldn't end up like her. I remember her saying to me that her counsellor had told her that above all else she must not purge. But I just couldn't allow myself to sit with all that food inside me. I could visualise the fat molecules coursing relentlessly through my blood stream, being absorbed by my fat cells and I would want to scream, head out of the house and run and run.

Every couple of days this routine would be repeated. Stuffing myself and then purging. Toilets of all descriptions became my ally. I knew that anyone who stayed in my parents' spare room would be able to hear me throwing up but I didn't care. I was numbed out on food most of the time and the remainder was spent starving myself and yearning for a way to lose weight.

I would swim for hours on end and go to the gym repeatedly, all to keep off the weight. Inevitably though, the measures weren't enough and my weight kept on creeping upwards. The old binges of my early teens which seemed bad enough at the time had turned into grotesque gorging sessions by the time I was 18. Bizarrely I never set out to binge; I was always trying to eat diet food. I couldn't understand why I would go from strict resolve to complete abandonment of all limits.

At my new school I was aware of at least six friends whose eating was disordered. Nicky, in my French class, suddenly and dramatically lost weight. She was anorexic and also engaged in bulimic episodes and was able to make herself vomit at will. She became so thin that she looked alarming. The skin on her face had that stretched, waxy, skeletal look with prominent nostrils, like the remains of preserved ancient Egyptians under their bandages. Bizarrely I was jealous of her for her appetite control and for being so thin. One morning I learned that she had drowned in her bath having passed out following an overdose of laxatives. I was to lose many friends and acquaintances to this deadly disease over the years.

My disease was progressing rapidly and my studies were badly affected. My teachers constantly compared me to my sister who had been at the school two years before me.

She had a happy disposition and worked hard. I felt thick and useless but I didn't really care too much as my disease had become a behemoth that had taken up residence in my head, leaving only a tiny portion of my mind free to think about anything else. When my A level English teacher announced to the whole class that our first essays had been an all-round disaster, I dropped the subject on the spot. She grabbed my arm, pulled me aside and berated me for my decision and asked me why wasn't I more like my sister. I looked straight through her and walked off.

Chapter 4: Appetite of an Ox

My A' level results were poor. I scraped a D for RE and an ordinary pass for French—in other words, I hadn't progressed at all. By the time I was 19 and attending the local technical college to learn typing and shorthand, not knowing what else to do, the bingeing was worse than ever. A typical binge would start with a crispbread with no intention whatever to have more than a couple. But, without fail, I would reach for another and another until the box was finished. The craving would then take over and I'd be on to slice after slice of bread, bowls of cereal with a cup of sugar on each, whole packs of biscuits, peanuts, jars of peanut butter, trifle, anything I could lay my hands on in the fridge and then I'd be off to the shops, going to different stores so they wouldn't think all the food was for me. I would binge on pastries, huge family-sized slabs of chocolate, bags of crisps and more biscuits as I drove along. My brain was wired and my hands shook as I tore open the packages. There was no satisfying the craving.

Stuffed to bursting and unable to eat a morsel more, I would pick a chemist I hadn't been to in a while to ask for laxatives suitable for children so they wouldn't think they were for me. Then I would get home and creep in unnoticed, feeling utterly disgusted with myself and depressed at what I knew I then had to do. I would lock myself in the bathroom, take my rings off and get on my hands and knees to throw up on the tiled floor as it was easier than leaning over the toilet. I would stick my fingers down my throat and use my stomach muscles at the same time to try to vomit up all the food. Sometimes I was successful but more often I couldn't throw up very much. If I'd eaten a massive amount of peanuts they would form a heavy layer in my stomach and vomiting was impossible despite using toothbrush handles to ram down my throat. Spitting out blood and stomach mucus and with bleeding knuckles, I would give up and lie down in extreme pain—screaming inside my head at the thought of the weight I'd be putting on.

If I was successful at throwing up, however, I would sense a surge of relief and cleansing. I would clean my teeth, scoop the slippery vomit off the floor with my bare hands and slop it into the toilet. This type of vomit has no smell as there's no bile involved; just sickly, greasy cake mixture with masses of stomach mucus. I would clean up the bathroom and look at my bloodshot eyes in the mirror say 'Showtime!'

to my reflection and head downstairs for a cup of tea and a cigarette.

On the times I'd also taken laxatives (over 100 at a time by this stage) then it would be a case of wondering when the stomach cramps would hit me. I knew the pain would be excruciating but I continued to believe that it would prevent weight gain. As ever, I would alternate between bouts of sitting on the toilet with explosive diarrhoea and lying on the floor grabbing hold of the toilet to stop myself screaming in pain or waiting for oblivion as I would pass out yet again from the effects of the laxatives.

A time came when my body rebelled against swallowing laxatives, however, and I would retch at the thought of the tablets or liquid paraffin that I used. In fact I could call to mind one particular laxative, Nylax, as an aid to help me vomit.

Fortunately I'd never heard of the emetic, Ipecac, the drug that caused Karen Carpenter's death by cardiac arrest. She took it in order to purge her binges not knowing that when used routinely, it weakens the heart muscle. Had I known there was a drug that caused vomiting I would have done anything to get my hands on it. I even seriously thought about getting hold of a stomach pump.

Like other addicts I stole. I stole food from my parents, friends and strangers. At my lowest, I stole the food meant for the children of a woman who had sought refuge with our family. Initially I stole from the box of food she kept in the kitchen for her daughters. She then put a sticker on it saying 'Jessie and Lucy's teatime bits and pieces'. It didn't deter me. Even when she hid the food in her bedroom, it still didn't deter me and I would rummage through her belongings to find the snacks while she was downstairs. My heart would pound for fear of being caught but, as only an addict will know, the craving obliterates all other thoughts and no sense of right or wrong can stop the compulsion to get and use the substance. Not even the mortifying realisation that she and my mother were fully aware of the stealing (and that my mother would write her cheques to compensate her) was enough to put me off.

By this stage there was nothing left of the anxious little girl with a mischievous streak. My mind had been hijacked by mental illness and obsession. There was virtually no space left to care for anyone, let alone myself. My only feelings of self-worth were tied to my appearance and body image. That was all that mattered and all I cared about. One of my sister's friends asked me if I was a model and her comment was the highlight of my life at that point. Whenever a man showed any interest in me or workmen wolf-whistled at me I was initially happy and then anxious, not knowing how long I could prevent weight gain by purging and starving. Sooner or later these same people might find me repulsive.

If a man wanted me, in whatever way, it meant I was still attractive. I was so anxious not to offend that on a few occasions in between longer-term relationships I let boy-friends sleep with me even though I didn't want to—never wanted to actually. I had absolutely no sex drive at the time but I liked the cuddles and kissing that went along with sex and the feeling of being desired for a brief moment. To please boyfriends I did things that made me feel sick and I let them hurt me—again because I didn't want to offend them. I'd heard of women feeling terrible after being used by men but the binges suppressed nearly all of my emotions and I felt virtually nothing after being used and thrown away. There were some feelings of rejection but they didn't last long though as I would soon be stuffing them down with food. I'd listen to Gladys Knight's version of *Help me make it through the night* as a kind of justification for my behaviour and self-pity

After my binges I would sit for hours talking with my mother, chain smoking and drinking tea. I couldn't under-stand my behaviour and why I couldn't stop eating. I didn't tell her about my purging but I thought she must have known. I didn't tell her about the boyfriends who used and hurt me. My mother would say, 'I know you'll find a solution one day'.

Later I found out that she had absolutely no idea I was purging, nor of the extent of my binges. My mother believed firmly in not interfering and allowing all of us to make our own way in life. My sister, I discovered only years later, had always worried about me and was fully aware of my behaviour. She had even cleared away bags of vomit and food remains from my bedroom cupboards. The state my bedroom was in used to frighten her. It wasn't just a messy bedroom, as any teenager might have, it was a wreck.

I had very little awareness or capacity to think about how my disease affected my family. I was in my own insane world, unable to see beyond myself and my obsessions. If there was no binge food in the house and I'd eaten all the drinking chocolate and Horlicks powder mixed to a paste with milk; or there was nothing for me to salvage from the dustbin and I had no cash or cheques on me; I would steal from my younger brother's pocket-money tin. It was a horrible thing to do but my conscience, along with all other feelings, was continually smothered by my gorging and then the craving for my next fix.

At the point when I was stealing from people who stayed with us, my family must have discussed strategies for dealing with my disease. On one occasion the food suddenly vanished from the larder. I was glad as I thought it would help prevent me from bingeing. But as with all addictions, the cravings soon set in. A short search later and I found my 'drugs' in the cupboard under the stairs. The next binge soon pre-empted any feelings of guilt and shame before they hit me.

By the time I was 20, I was bingeing every other day and was unable to hold down a job for longer than about a month. As an antidote, I had the idea that I would try nursing and applied to Orpington Hospital for my training. I was excited at the prospect and felt that this might cure me of my bulimia. I reasoned that to get a job caring for others might be what I needed to get away from my extreme obsession with myself which my mother very kindly had helped me to see. I was accepted on to the course and moved into the nurses' residence.

I started my training and was enjoying my studies and interacting with the other students. But after just a week I was back to my old ways. This time however, I couldn't rely on my parents' constant supply of food. I had to try to make my tiny salary pay for my disordered eating. So I started stealing again. I stole bread and cereal from the other students who shared the block with me. I stole food from the ward kitchens and stole chocolates and sweets from patients' lockers. A large proportion of the patients on the ward had advanced dementia so it was easy to pick on the most vulnerable who couldn't communicate and probably wouldn't notice that I had stolen their sweets anyway. However, the amount I was able to get my hands on just wasn't enough. I would drive around after my shifts buying hamburgers and other junk food, taking it back to my room to binge on in secret. I would then vomit into bin bags and tie up the bags ready to take them out and hide them among the rubbish.

Still I couldn't get enough food so I would go out in the early hours driving to garages for more. Once, at around three o'clock in the morning, I drove back to my parents' house and let myself in as quietly as I could. I went straight to the kitchen and started to stuff my face with anything I could lay my hands on. My father is a light sleeper, however, and I don't know how long he was standing there but I suddenly noticed him in the doorway. I felt sick with guilt and disgust at myself. I stood there ashamed and unable to speak.

I remember him saying something like, 'We are just like Jane's mother and father; we have a daughter with a terminal illness'. (Jane was a close friend from school who had died of cancer at 16). My father knew my disease was deadly serious long before I did.

I carried on working at the hospital for another month but moved back home as I couldn't face the guilt of stealing from other nurses' lockers. I hoped I would still be able to complete my training but with support from home. However, the bingeing continued to worsen and I finally spoke to one of my tutors to let her know of my issues. She said to me that I should leave and that I shouldn't try to train again until I had been binge-free for two years. However, she did ask me to work out a notice period of four weeks. I had a holiday booked and said that I would return to complete it. Once on holiday, I decided I couldn't face going back and asked my friend to phone up the hospital to say I wouldn't be returning. I lasted only six months into my training.

On holiday I felt free again and managed a week without a single binge until the first rainy day. There was no more sunbathing and showing off my tan and recent weight loss. What happened in my brain at that point I have no idea but I headed to the supermarket with one intention: to eat. I didn't want my friend to see me so I stuffed my face on the journey back to the apartment. I locked myself in the bathroom and tried to throw up all the food but wasn't very successful. The weather perked up again quickly and for the remainder of the vacation I was able to starve myself.

Back from holiday in the miserable damp climate at home, the bingeing became horrific again. I had read that I could endanger my life and rupture my stomach but I was able to put the thought out of my mind and gorge. My car became my bingeing parlour and I would drive around wired, bingeing my brains out and endangering the lives of others as I drove erratically from one shop to the next. I was able to forge my mother's signature and would take her credit card to the supermarket on the pretext of doing the shopping for her. I would buy a few items for the home and masses of binge foods which I'd eat before arriving home. I'd put the few bits of food away in the cupboard and—knowing that time was ticking and that my body would be starting to digest the food—I would stagger upstairs and go through the purging ritual.

I went on another holiday the same summer and as before I managed a few days in the new environment without bingeing. But before long I would be off to the shops to binge. On one particular evening I locked myself in the bathroom and binged but I was unable to make myself vomit. Panicking, I made a conscious decision to drink to excess so that I would throw up and not put on too much weight. I drank Malibu and pineapple cocktails in succession, had a huge dinner, and drank wine, spirits and anything I could get my hands on. It worked. I remember lying naked in the hotel bath covered in vomit and not really caring that friends were coming in to the bathroom to take photos of me in this state. I spent the night crying and wailing and telling everyone I'd caused the death of my friend, Jane, who I had encouraged to smoke after she was in remission from cancer. I believed that the lung metastases she had developed were a direct result of my influence.

The next morning with a pounding head I went outside and dived into the deep end of the swimming pool thinking it would refresh me and sober me up. The shock of it was paralysing. I lay at the bottom believing this was the end of me and wondered how much I'd suffer. Then utter panic set in and somehow I managed to will myself to move and desperately aim for the surface. I fought and fought to break out into fresh air and some strangers, who must have seen me struggling, pulled me out to the side of the pool.

When I got back from the holiday, the bingeing revved up a gear and the weight I'd lost on holiday started to pile back on again. I got a job as a receptionist not knowing what else I could do. It was about this time that I started going out with a friend I'd known for a year or so, after his friends had told me he'd fancied me for ages. Neil had been in a long-term relationship and up until that point I hadn't considered him as boyfriend material. However, I felt confident enough to flirt with him and not long afterwards he broke up with his girlfriend and we started seeing each other. Neil was tall, well-built and wonderful to cuddle. With his friend, Steve, he was one half of a comedy duo in our circle of friends. The laughter and affection gave me some moments of happiness and hope and a chance to forget my eating disorder for a short while.

In the autumn, I had a brief scare in hospital where I had exploratory operations on both breasts so that biopsies could be performed on the lumps I'd discovered. It was when the first campaigns came out to be breast aware and if it had been today rather than 1987 I would have been scanned rather than opened up under general anaesthetic. Bizarrely, I was glad I was going to have the operations and was binge free for nearly two weeks. After the operation Neil proposed to me and I was so happy that I felt I would never over-eat again.

Shortly afterwards I was back in hospital as an abscess had formed in the wound of one of my breasts. My right breast swelled up like a watermelon and a satisfyingly disgusting, pea-soup-like pus started to pour out of the wound. I had an operation to have the wound drained and then packed with caustic swabs for several days. I hadn't cried for years—not since I was a child—but on my bed in that ward I cried and cried. Silent tears streamed down my face for several hours. I didn't feel sad, it just felt like an emotional outpouring and afterwards I felt saner than I had done in years.

A few days out of hospital, however, and the bingeing came back with a ferocity that scared the living daylights out of me. I decided to tell Neil that I had a problem with compulsive eating but didn't go into much detail. He said he'd noticed my weight yo-yo-ing and I felt ashamed. All my binges and purges were in secret and I was sure my closest friends didn't know.

Perhaps to compensate for how much I loathed myself on the inside, I used to take hours getting ready before going out. My make-up had to be just right and my clothes were either black and baggy, if I felt fat, or figure-hugging, if I felt slim. I was a chronic people-pleaser too and all my motives were driven by wanting to be liked, desired or approved of. Outwardly I thought I looked happy, confident and glamorous, but inwardly I had my shameful, sordid and disgusting secret. It was a great big act and I was leading a dual life.

I stayed with Neil a few days a week and at my parents' house for the remainder. Neil had bought a house with his friend Pete and when I stayed over I was unable to control myself and would steal Pete's food and deny I'd taken it. Pete had confronted Neil about it but I think he shielded me from the criticism.

Just before the Easter weekend, his girlfriend had put a Cadbury's Chocolate Buttons egg in the fridge. When I saw it in the fridge my mind screamed 'EAT NOW'. I wrestled with the idea but very soon my addict's brain had come up with a plan. I reasoned I could open the egg carefully, take off the foil, separate the two halves of the egg and take out the bag of chocolate buttons in the middle. Mission accomplished, I stuck the egg halves back together by heating a knife and running it around the rim of one half of the egg, wrapped it up and put it back in the fridge. On Easter day I groaned inwardly as Pete's girlfriend unwrapped the egg and discovered the missing chocolate buttons. She looked straight at me and my cheeks burned with guilt. In denial, I said to her that she should complain to Cadbury's. I felt a bit better when she told me later she'd written to complain and received a box full of eggs and other confectionery from the manufacturer.

In winter, with a snowfall that was up to my armpits in places, cars abandoned and useless, I traipsed for miles in the snow to find a shop that was open so that I could get my stash of binge foods. The force of the craving put all thoughts of the freezing discomfort out of my mind. I stuffed myself behind a bus shelter where I thought I couldn't be seen. Because my fingers were too numb to help me throw up, I traipsed all the way back in extreme discomfort from my distended stomach with one thought on my mind; to purge.

It wasn't as easy to manage my binges at Neil and Pete's house and so most took place when I was back at my parents' home but I would often return to Neil's after a binge and would have to throw up there. It was a typical bachelor pad and the small toilet had urine-soaked carpet around the pubic-hair-encrusted pedestal. When I needed to purge it was no deterrent and I would be on all fours wrapped around the toilet trying to rid myself of the junk food I'd gorged on. In fact the smell of the toilet helped me to gag and retch.

For Neil, the only thing that seemed to bother him was when my weight went up. He would grab hold of the fat on my hips and wobble it up and down telling me I was wearing my jelly jodhpurs again. He did it in a teasing way rather than a harsh way but I still felt upset. He would lose interest in sex and I'd feel worthless. When my weight went down, he would find me attractive again and sex was back on the agenda.

At work I was even unable to control my eating there and would steal food from the supply cupboard. Eventually, because of the time I was away from my desk, I was given a verbal warning. Ashamed, I handed in my resignation and left.

Chapter 5: Dying to Recover

This was my life for years: obsessed with weight and appearance, obsessed with food. I was unable to see past my self-centredness or to see the pain and hurt I was causing everyone around me. I was living like a parasite in my parents' home, unable to hold down a job. My moods swung between despair and massive surges of hope that I would one day find a cure. But the hope (the wretched hope) was the most devastating part of it because it was always dashed with the next binge.

I had no understanding of why I did what I did. Why I felt compelled to stuff myself to bursting point, to steal food from home, friends and strangers. Why did I engage in this utter insanity and then the desperate acts that followed to avoid putting on weight? Purging—through inducing vomiting or taking hundreds of laxatives in the mistaken belief that it would prevent weight gain—is at best unpleasant and at worst excruciating and life threatening.

Bulimia—I hated that f***ing word. I despised myself and my sordid secret. I despaired at the relentless cycle of starving for days then stealing, gorging, purging, running or swimming for hours on end to avoid weight gain. Almost as bad was the horrific waste of time and life it all entailed. I hated that and the superficiality of focusing entirely on body image and the pursuits of being thin and then blowing it all by bingeing my brains out anyway. I was desperate to find a way out, this was slow suicide and for me my only options were to recover or to end it all quickly.

I sought out my GP to see what help might be on offer. The first doctor I saw told me I was a bit sad but not depressed. He patted me on the hand, told me I was an attractive young woman and that I should go out and enjoy myself. I booked another appointment with a different GP and was referred to a clinical psychologist immediately. He asked me a string of questions. One that stuck in my mind and seemed rather random was to ask me why I hadn't plucked my eyebrows to a thin line but I never did find out the relevance. I was referred to a Freudian-style therapist who believed that sex was the answer to all my problems. It seemed to me to be absurdly naive to suggest sex as the cure via the prescription of a book on the subject. I didn't bother going back and didn't bother getting the book.

The next therapist was recommended by friends of my parents. Annie was very kind but really didn't get my problem. She said to me that becoming interested in a career would stop me worrying about food and weight. I went for two sessions but felt no benefit and didn't bother returning. She was the type of therapist perfectly suited to normal people with a few emotional issues. I just couldn't see how I could even think about a career when I wasn't even able to hold down a basic job. My life was completely out of control and my disease was far too big for her to handle.

After that I tried two sessions with a medium who looked like she had a severe problem with food herself. She had a beautiful, James Bond-style Persian cat with a dirty bottom who insisted on sitting on my lap. She did the typical medium routine, 'I'm getting the letter K, does that mean anything to you?'

I racked my brain to think of someone I knew whose name began with the letter K. I eventually settled on my grandparents' next door neighbour, who I'd never met. I tried very hard to make it fit but it just seemed ridiculous. Her idea of treatment was to encourage me to become a gourmet with both food *and* sex. With food I was to start by creating the most amazing and adventurous sandwich and then move on to more challenging dishes. For the sex part, I was to encourage Neil to read a book on the art of lovemaking. It all seemed so absurd. These people just didn't get the severity of my disease. Needless to say I didn't return. Though I didn't know it at the time I was in the same critical condition as a heroin addict; I needed to get and stay clean.

My next encounter was with a hypnotherapist who rented an office in a nursing home. My mother came with me and I remember how strange it felt waiting in the television lounge watching the quiz show, Blockbusters, with all the residents before my appointment. The hypnotherapist was an odd character and always wore a safari suit with leopard print cravats. The first thing he told me was that only intelligent people could be hypnotised. He then started his routine, counting down from ten to one, telling me I was beginning to feel sleepy and that by the time he reached one I would be under his control. He then said in a dramatic voice, 'No one else [theatrical pause] will ever have [another pause] any power over you other than me'. The words, 'Complete bollocks' came to mind, but being obsessed with my appearance, both physically and intellectually, I didn't want him to think I was too stupid to be hypnotised so I hung my head as if in a trance and pretended.

Unsurprisingly, it was a totally useless exercise and very painful to sit and fake being in a trance for so long. He must have believed I was genuinely hypnotised as he spent a long time with his hand down the back of his trousers scratching his bottom. I told him he'd cured me after three sessions and cancelled the remainder.

The next therapist I saw had been recommended to me by my sister as her friend suffered from the same condition as me. This practitioner told me that she had never seen someone with so much self-hatred and that I would require intensive therapy several times a week. I felt a strange kind of pride to be told how much I hated myself. As each session would cost over £100, however, this was out of the question for my parents to afford back then.

A few months later, I started to see a practitioner who had set up an eating disorders centre in the West End. Her theory, still popular today, was that those who denied themselves certain foods would ultimately binge on them. She kept fashion magazines for the larger lady in her waiting room but was herself emaciated. She dressed like one of the leading ladies in the television series, Dallas, complete with big hair and shoulder pads. She told me to set myself free from restraint and eat what my body 'told' me to—so called 'intuitive eating'. This very rapidly led to one of the worst periods of bingeing and purging in my life—when I listened to my body it told me to binge my brains out. Little did I know, then, that this was the same misguided advice as those practitioners who tell an alcoholic that they should restrict their drinking to one small glass every day. Ask any recovering alcoholic and they'll tell you there is no such thing as one sip, let alone one glass. I went back to see her without much hope but as I'd already paid for the session I thought I would keep it anyway. While I was waiting for my appointment I heard someone throwing up in the toilet. She came out dabbing her mouth with a tissue and I knew then for sure that her theory was as flimsy as she was.

Finally, in April 1987 aged 21, I saw an advert in one of the free job magazines (Ms London) that was out at the time. It read 'Psychotherapy for Compulsive Food Addicts'. I was stunned. Here was a label that finally fitted me. I phoned up for an appointment immediately but after a day or so I wavered and cancelled. One horrific binge later and I called again to make another appointment and this time I kept it.

Part II

Chapter 6: The Ferryman

If you can imagine, Narnia-style, a portal suddenly opens and you step through blinking into an amazing paradise full of rich colours, vibrancy and life. But this paradise, you discover, is actually the real world. You can't stay here though, but you're allowed a glimpse. Back through the portal to where you've been for an eternity there is nothing but self-centredness and greed. In this world you're alone among a multitude of others. It's full of piles of greasy, stodgy food, there's filth and empty wrappers, shit- and vomit-stained clothes and sheets lying everywhere. Ugly people who think they look glamorous wander around vacantly looking for a reflection of themselves in shiny surfaces and other people's eyes. It's full of distorting mirrors and sometimes you're enchanted by your appearance and at other times you're horrified. You swing from wailing at your lot in this hole to short bursts of feeling a blissful numbness for a few minutes while you gorge on junk food. But there's no escape from yourself or this place. Then the ferryman appears with his cargo of children and offers to take you back the other way—if you're willing to pay the price.

* * *

On first meeting the man who was to become my therapist, I felt very uneasy but compelled to sit and listen as he began to tell me what I had waited nearly all my life to hear—that there was no chance I would ever eat normally because I was a food addict and needed radical treatment. The solution, he said, would lie in a food plan and a course of therapy and that I would have to be prepared to go to any lengths to recover. I asked him how long it would take and he said it would take about three years of intense therapy. As I sat there taking in his radical methods I couldn't have imagined the paradox that would unfold—the startling recovery from my food addiction but at an incredible personal, emotional and financial cost to me and my family.

I would experience the indescribable joy and freedom from bulimia, but 23 years of enslavement by someone who had become a cult-like guru. At one stage he said that he had forty clients all over the UK. He would hold sessions in North Wales, Sheffield, Cambridge, Eastbourne and London. Though I occasionally passed one or two of his other clients in corridors while waiting for my therapy sessions, I was expressly forbidden to look at or talk to any of them.

He came across as believing he was the ultimate in moral and spiritual authority. Without a shadow of a doubt he saved my life and taught me so much, but he became my master and my gaoler. His ruthless pursuit of spiritual perfection justified the brutal regime he ultimately forced on me as well as the heartache and loss of being separated from family and friends. I was utterly dependent on him for all but the most basic decisions of daily life and it was a gruelling and at times harrowing existence as I was to embrace sleep deprivation, psychological torture, verbal abuse, endless solitude and brain washing.

* * *

My new therapist introduced me to the food plan. It was a reasonably healthy plan consisting of a balance of protein, vegetables, fruit, healthy fats and complex carbs together with total abstinence from binge trigger foods. The latter include all forms of sugar, flour, wheat, nuts and high animal fat. All labels on food were to be scrutinized carefully for any trigger ingredients and all of my food portions were to be weighed and measured. I bought kitchen scales and measuring cups and spoons and started on the plan. He explained that he would control my body weight by weighing me every week and would adjust my portions to keep my weight within certain parameters.

It worked like magic. I had no cravings for binge foods. I weighed and measured my meals and kept strictly to the plan without deviating. Twenty-eight years later I still weigh and measure my food and abstain from addictive trigger foods. I've been free of food addiction ever since.

Things that normal eaters would take for granted had me floating around in a state of extreme joy. My kitchen cupboards and my fridge were stocked full of healthy food where previously they would have been empty apart from some rotting but well-intentioned salad and a car or bedroom full of binge detritus.

I was beyond happy and I was ready to do anything to keep hold of my newly found freedom from this mental illness. I didn't care that my therapist would control my weight and keep it above the weight I wanted it to be. I didn't know then, however, that he would keep on increasing my weight further and further.

My therapist explained to me that my disease was twofold, that I was addicted to food as well as to appearances which included both my body image as well as how I perceived I came across to others. This all made complete sense to me given my obsession with the bathroom scales and the time I spent in front of the mirror applying my make-up or scrutinising my body for imperfections. It made sense in terms of how I would groan to myself as I would replay interactions with others in my head wishing I could change what I'd said or done.

So while the food plan took care of my food addiction, my 'appearance addiction' had to be dealt with too. My weight was set at a level that meant I was what most would consider overweight; this was known as my surrender weight. From that point on I was to wear only second hand clothes and was no longer permitted to wear make-up or jewellery. I had to opt out of the appearance race and the term 'opted out' became an expression that was to be drummed into me time after time.

I found out why I was never to speak to or look at his other clients. He said it was to prevent us making comparisons with each other which would fuel the obsession with our appearance.

According to my therapist, now that the 'cork was back in the bottle'—as far as food and appearance addiction were concerned—the therapy work could begin. As with many forms of traditional psychotherapy, it took a cruelly anti-parent stance. I was to spend the first few years going over my childhood hurts, to cry for the 'inner child' who had been 'abused and neglected' by her parents and this would then set me on the path of healing.

Chapter 7: Psychotherapy

I was made to think back over my childhood experiences to try to uncover any festering wounds that needed excising and healing. I would rake around in my memory to recall incidents that I thought would fit the bill; but it wasn't easy. He told me that this was evidence of my denial over my parents' treatment of me. I told him how strict my father had been and about the smacks we got but he seemed disappointed that I wasn't coming up with anything serious.

I described how my mother was always late picking me up from school, drama, ballet or oboe lessons. This, he believed, was a strong indicator of my mother's lack of genuine love for me. However, with four children and a hectic schedule I'm not surprised she was late and it wasn't as if I was singled out for such treatment.

He asked about hugs and affection from my parents and I could recall the hugs we all had together from time to time and the song that accompanied them. We had what we called lions' day on Sunday mornings when my dad would go on all fours, chase us around the house, catch us and pretend to maul us. I remembered the smell of my dad's clothes, always clean and with a light scent of his aftershave and recalled how I liked to put on his jumpers as they made me feel snug and secure. He had big, strong hands and I loved it when he held mine as we walked along. I remembered a few specific occasions of having hugs from my mother but they would have been so frequent that I couldn't possibly remember every one. There was always a good night kiss and my mother used to like to bite my nose affectionately. As I recalled my memories I didn't feel any fear or pain but plenty of warm feelings towards my family. However, my therapist would simply say that this was further evidence of my being in denial. And the more he told me I was in denial the more I started to wonder whether he might be right and that I had been neglected. There was something very appealing about the idea of being a victim and of having someone to blame for my behaviour.

One particular time that did have me sobbing in my therapy session was when I described a relatively recent incident of visiting a rare animal farm with Neil. We were in the sheep enclosure and a lamb was frantically running away from all the people who wanted to pet her. Then a mother and father wheeled their severely disabled son in to the middle of the enclosure in his wheel chair. The lamb came running up to the little boy and nuzzled against him;

letting him caress her beautifully soft, woolly head. A huge smile lit up the boy's face and I couldn't hold back my tears. To me it seemed like an indication of the presence of something special in this world. My therapist said that, rather, it was connected to the lamb we had as a pet for a while but ultimately had to give to friends who owned a smallholding.

I didn't agree with his analysis as I remember the whole family had felt it was the right decision for Winnie to be moved to a more suitable home rather than the small enclosure in the garden of our suburban house in Orpington. I don't remember any sadness at the time but my therapist decided it was a momentous incident and the start of tapping in to long-buried emotions.

What the incident did call to mind was my neglect of my rabbits and guinea pigs as a child. I left them cold and hungry in dirty hutches because I was too lazy to clean them out as frequently as I should have. They often had no hay left in their cages as they would eat all their bedding. By the time I cleaned them out, maggots were starting to hatch in their droppings at the bottom of the hutch. They were lucky if they were fed every day rather than every other day and I would leave notes at night time asking my mother to feed them. I didn't notice them drink so I decided not to put a water bottle in their cages. Instead they had to survive on the juice in the carrots, fruit and vegetable peelings I fed them on. It was the start of many recurring nightmares about neglecting animals and I still feel the pain of the harm

I caused them today. I wish I could go back in time and undo all the suffering.

As I thought about these incidents, other animal-connected memories came to mind. I remembered the two occasions my father had had to put down a mouse and a hamster when they were very sick. The method he used was quick but gruesome. I also recalled my older brother's treatment of his pets. My father had bought him a King snake that had to be fed live mice. It upset my brother too much to watch the mice being constricted and swallowed live so he let the mice loose in the house instead and the snake starved to death. Another time, I remembered bringing a pigeon with a broken wing indoors and putting it in a hay-lined box in my bedroom. Later on that day I discovered the pigeon was gone from my room and I found my older brother in the garden with a rope around its neck trying to put it out of its misery.

I then recalled an incident at a farm we visited while on another camping holiday in France. The whole family stood around cooing while a farmer held a large white rabbit on his lap and stroked it. Looking up at us with a smile, he pulled a penknife out of his pocket and started cutting into the rabbit's neck behind its ears. The rabbit took a long time to die. My sister, brother and I looked on screaming and my parents were frozen to the spot in horror. I didn't know rabbits could scream too.

Ever since I recalled these painful memories, whenever I saw cruelty to animals on the television or elsewhere I would feel utterly traumatised. A colleague at work told me about a programme she'd seen where a cat had been skinned alive for the fur trade in China; she described the poor animal quivering where it stood afterwards. I rushed to the disabled toilet, locked the door, curled into a ball, rammed my jumper into my mouth and screamed and screamed. I just couldn't shake the image that had built up in my mind and I was distraught for days. Another time I saw a man kicking his dog in the street near where I lived. I ran up to him and pleaded with him to stop. He stopped initially then swore at me and carried on kicking his dog even harder. I ran home crying my eyes out.

My therapist would say that my overreaction to seeing animal cruelty was indicative of the hurts inside me from my childhood and that they had found an outlet through my bond with animals. I became more and more convinced that he was right. The reality was, I was no longer anaesthetised by my drugs and so I had to deal with real raw emotions which had surfaced as a result of digging around in my memory.

My therapist concluded that my mother was the direct cause of my bulimia. I never did work out how he made the leap between traumatic experiences with animals and my mother's treatment of me though. He vilified her as an emotional vampire who was desperate to be needed by her children and had a vested interest in keeping us psychologically ill. She had her emotional hooks in me, apparently, and fed off my mental illness. She wanted me to be sick so I would need her forever yet at the same time was unable to provide for my emotional needs. I remember arguing with him and saying how much I adored her as a child but he said that my feelings for her were indicative of the emotional ties she held me with. Such was her judgement.

My father, on the other hand, was described as a harsh but indifferent parent; culpable in so far as his physical punishments were handed out but too self-centred to have had as great an impact as my mother apparently had. He was, however, part of our apparently dysfunctional family unit and therefore a danger to my recovery.

In fact, according to my therapist, 90% of all humans are 'sick'. It was the term he used to describe all those who didn't follow a Christ-like life of self-sacrifice and suffering. The remaining ten per cent included him and a few fortunate others. Those of us who were his clients were aspiring 'ten per centers'. The more he drummed his theories into me, then, the more I began to believe I was superior to most because I was now living a 'spiritual' life. How I thought I was in a position to look down on anyone else given my background was astonishing.

As the unfortunate saying goes, to boil a frog you have to start with a pan of cold water. Such was the process of brainwashing which led me to reject a short lifetime of belief in my parents' values to the complete transference of allegiance to my therapist's philosophy. The psychological bars that would hold me captive for so many years were being relentlessly and ruthlessly forged. But here, again, a paradox: this man had saved my life, had transformed me from being a self-destructive, self-obsessed zombie, to becoming an exceptionally diligent and hard-working person. He instilled in me the critical self-discipline I had always lacked. And not just for me, he said he had enabled countless women to be free of the slavery of food addiction. With such a transformation and the knowledge that of all mental illnesses, eating disorders have the highest mortality rate[2], why wouldn't I believe he didn't speak the truth on every subject? Why wouldn't I trust him and do everything I was told?

He said that by distancing ourselves from our families we were actually doing them a huge favour by giving them the space to look at their own shortcomings and seek professional help. Indeed, to do anything else would be tantamount to abusing them given our 'superior' insight.

I started to feel so special and spiritual. It was, of course, a pseudo-spirituality as my therapist had become my god, but I felt like I was part of something really powerful—powerful enough to change lives. I now fully believed I'd suffered as a child and that this had caused my food addiction.

He told me I was one of the loveliest people he'd ever met and I felt completely accepted. I remember sitting in his office one Sunday thinking to myself, 'I'm so happy, I could die right here and right now and it would be perfect'. I'm sure a similar approach is used by extremists and cults to recruit the 'fallen' but this was supercharged as it was underpinned by the fact that he had saved my life. For those of us whose lives had lost their meaning, whose lives had become out of control and who were spiralling downwards towards complete self-destruction, this was redemption.

Chapter 8: Leaving Home

Tensions were very apparent between my parents and me and I think my mother, in particular, must have sensed my feelings towards her had changed as she seemed distant. Given my appearance, I felt that she also disapproved of my clothes and my size. I moved into a flat with Neil in Tonbridge and saw less and less of my parents over the next few months as I became increasingly convinced by what my therapist was telling me about the cause of my bulimia.

Adapting to wearing no make-up and second hand clothes wasn't easy but I was euphoric about being abstinent. When Neil first met me I would spend hours getting ready and was always fully made up and fashionably dressed. By this time I was buying my clothes from charity shops and wearing tracksuit bottoms and sweatshirts around the house. I became quite evangelistic about the superficiality of appearances and would happily preach to people if I was asked about my clothes. Deep down, though,

I felt inferior and jealous of others. Neil didn't say anything to start with but gradually started to tell me stories about how he'd heard of other women giving up on themselves. He said how wonderful it was when he heard of one woman who would get up an hour before her partner to do her hair and make-up before he woke up. I wished I could still dress up for Neil but the miracle of being binge free for six months meant that I was prepared to do anything to safeguard my precious recovery.

Neil's mother was concerned about the change in my appearance too and sent me a letter encouraging me to dress attractively for Neil and suggested that it was a waste of my looks not to enhance them. It seemed such an innocent thing to say but given the recovery I'd experienced with my therapist and my total obsession with my appearance throughout my bulimic years I was convinced by my therapist's theory. I tried to explain that for normal people (i.e. those who didn't have an eating disorder) it was fine to dress up and look good, but it wasn't okay for me. But I just couldn't make anyone understand.

My therapist knew nothing of the conversations I had about my looks and I let him believe that Neil was supportive. He said that as I hadn't been in the relationship for that long it would be okay for me to go ahead with the wedding. As Neil had asked me to marry him I think he must have felt obliged to see it through and I was too ashamed to ask if he felt differently now. I thought back to when he had proposed to me—in bed after sex when I was slim and wearing white silk underwear. I remembered the evening we spent together feeling elated, looking into each other's eyes, drunk with happiness and calling people randomly to share the news.

I ploughed ahead with the wedding plans despite my misgivings. I was concerned about what I could wear, given that my clothes were supposed to be opted-out. I decided to find something from a fairly down-market local wedding-dress shop as a compromise. I chose a white satin dress with an oyster-coloured sheen, a short veil and flowered tiara. I would carry a bouquet of the most exquisite bridal roses and gypsophila that my mother and sister had ordered for me at the florist. On the day, I got dressed up and risked wearing make-up and getting my hair done. Unfortunately my fringe was cut too short and my French pleat was unflattering and so I felt self-conscious.

When we stepped out of the chapel after the ceremony Neil joked that I looked like a fat fairy. It smarted but I laughed it off and gave him a hug. I smiled and smiled as I greeted the guests for the reception but my cheeks ached from the effort and I wanted it all to be over. At the hotel afterwards Neil looked at my hair and joked, 'Not tonight Josephine', turned over and was soon asleep.

* * *

I visited my therapist three times a week initially and remember sitting in the cramped, windowless room in an office block in Vauxhall for my therapy sessions. I think it must have been previously the cleaning supplies room as it could just about fit his desk, diagonally placed, with a chair either side. A ceramic figurine of a child nestled in a dismembered hand sat on the desk and there was a tea-towel pinned to the door with the 'Nun's prayer'[a] on it.

My therapist smelled strongly of coal tar soap and had a squeaky fan on at all times. He was just over 5ft tall with a large frame and broad shoulders. He wore large boots with built up heels and had a salt-and-pepper beard that hid most of his face and neck. His eyes were dark and penetrating with vivid contrasting whites. He had a booming voice with a clipped British accent and an air of absolute authority.

I remember he would ask me how I had been since my last session and about my relationship with Neil. Then the moment I would dread as he would ask if we'd been making love regularly. I would cringe inside and blush outwardly. He said that it was critical to ask me to ensure all was well with our relationship. I remember feeling desperately embarrassed as he would probe and dig to find out exactly what we did to each other and would then tell me what we should and shouldn't do in bed; condemning certain practises such as foreplay. He would say 'Don't let Neil maaasturbate you' elongating the first vowel as in the word 'plaster' and I would squirm in absolute horror and hope for a quick, painless death. He would ask if my periods were regular and whether my 'cerverical' smear tests were up to date, always mispronouncing the word 'cervical' which somehow made it even more mortifying. I didn't feel he was a pervert, just monumentally embarrassing.

Neil was pleased that I had become a far happier and more emotionally stable partner and that I was finally able to hold down a job. However, the inconvenience of the food plan and how this affected our social life became a source of annoyance for him as did my appearance of course. He once said to me, 'I feel like I've been sold a dud. I thought I was marrying the girl I first met and then someone took her away and replaced her with you'. We started to argue and I believed he was a danger to my recovery.

Having kept to myself the arguments between us, I finally told my therapist about them. Initially he told me that I should refuse to sleep with Neil unless he went to therapy himself. He did see a therapist with my mother but they were both insulted by her. Neil was told he was weak and my mother was told that she was to blame for my eating disorder because she went on a diet after she was pregnant with my younger brother. One thing's for sure, I didn't even notice when my mother was on a diet and with her old nylon slacks and bright red, baggy acrylic jumper that she wore around the house I'm pretty sure she didn't trigger the obsession with my appearance. This therapist, the most well-known in her field at the time, told my mother and husband to forget me and move on with their lives.

My own therapist then decided that Neil would never change and said that sooner or later I would need to leave him and that he had a flat I could move into. I discussed the potential of a trial separation with Neil and told him that there was a flat in London I could rent for a short while from the company I worked for. I embellished the lie by saying I'd been told I could work from their London office during the time and this seemed a fairly plausible reason. I knew that I couldn't tell the truth about the flat being provided by my therapist of course—it would sound too dodgy. The conversation enraged Neil and in his frustration he threw a bottle of vitamins at the lounge door, making a hole in the cheap plywood. I ran into the bedroom and lay on the bed crying. He followed me in, raining punches down around me on the bed but never touching me. I didn't bring the subject up again until the day I was told I must pack my things and leave or risk losing my life.

One Saturday afternoon while Neil was playing cricket, I drove to work and left notes on my colleagues' desks to let them know I was leaving my husband and needed to get away from Tonbridge and that as a result I wouldn't be returning to work. I left a note for a close colleague, Cathy, to wish her well as she was expecting her first child. I apologised to my boss for having to leave so abruptly and without notice.

Early the next day I packed clothes, grabbed a duvet, my kitchen scales and some food and put our two cats into baskets. Neil woke up and came out pleading with me not to go. He hugged me and I agreed I'd just go and have a look at the flat and would return home that evening. He seemed reassured and left for his cricket match. I called my therapist and he said I must leave instantly. I put the cats back into their baskets and into the car, wrote a quick note to Neil and left with the items I'd packed previously.

I was on my way to a flat in east London that belonged (by virtue of a housing association), to one of my therapist's clients. I was crying so much as I drove up to London that I could hardly see. As I got to Stoke Newington I struggled to find the flat, driving the wrong way up one way streets and narrowly missing other cars.

Finally I found the road and after driving up and down for a while, spotted my therapist standing outside. The flat was part of a converted Victorian terraced house. Inside, it looked like it hadn't been touched since the 70s. In the lounge, the furniture, curtains and carpets were covered in feathers, bird droppings and birdseed. Throughout the flat, the yellowing wallpaper was peeling off the crumbling plaster. The kitchen was dirty with black mould up the walls, ceiling and in the fridge. A small plaque on one wall read, 'Today well lived, makes every yesterday a dream of happiness and every tomorrow a vision of hope.' This would be my home for the next 23 years.

My therapist sat with me and told me that my tears (which hadn't stopped since I left my home) were not because I was sad to leave but because I felt sorry for Neil. He told me that I'd be happily married again by the time I was 28 (I was 23 at the time). He carried on talking but I tuned out. I was thinking about my husband and how I loved him but knew that our relationship was doomed from the start. I definitely wasn't the same person he had first met and had I been brave enough, perhaps I would have ended the relationship for his sake.

I had been a very passive partner while I was in the thick of my disease but was becoming more assertive and decisive as my recovery progressed. However, I clung on to the comfort I got from the child-like affection we had for each other. We talked in silly voices and had a make-believe world that we often escaped to. He would insist on biting my nose (as my mother had done) and would lie on top of me on the floor, telling me I needed to be squashed. I loved it and I'd be laughing helplessly and hysterically under his weight. For 30% of the time, we had been very happy. He didn't understand the importance of my food plan but I had no doubts that it was critical and that without my recovery I would lose him anyway.

My therapist's voice brought me back to the present. He told me to call him at midnight from the call box near the station and then left. I sat on the dirty sofa looking down at the horrible patterns on the carpet. The cats were stressed and their behaviour was odd. They sat motionless together, both had one foreleg raised up and pressed against the wall.

I got up and had a look around and noticed that two rooms had been locked with a padlock: one was up a small flight of stairs and the other down in the basement. In the bathroom next door to the locked basement room, someone had tried to do a DIY makeover by badly painting the grouting with dark blue paint which had dribbled all over the tiles and dried. There were polystyrene picture rails hanging down half stuck on and unpainted. The boiler was broken so there was no hot water and the flat had no central heating; just a condemned gas heater in the lounge.

A flight of wooden stairs led from the kitchen down to the garden which was level with the basement. The garden was overgrown and piled with bricks and rubble and had a low wall running around it.

Over and over in my mind I kept telling myself I was doing the right thing; that this was a means to a new life. I was leaving Neil and my family because they were a threat to my recovery and while it seemed very harsh, I was told I was leaving them in a spirit of tough love, just as when Christ told his followers that they should, 'Leave the dead to bury their own dead'[3]. Very fortunately I had no children or I would have been forced to leave them too as several of the women under my therapist's control had been made to do.

I cried myself to sleep that night. My cats were perched like sitting hens on my chest and stomach, swaying slightly as I breathed in and out. They were a huge source of comfort then and through the years to come. Looking back, I think I went into a kind of psychological shock—an almost trance-like state that would keep me protected over the years.

Chapter 9: Easing in to Purgatory

The next day I called my mother to let her know I was okay. It was an awkward conversation where she said that my father had called my company to be told they had nothing to do with the flat. I ended the call quickly. I felt bad but at the same time I was certain that my family would do anything to try and stop me because they didn't understand the severity of my disease. When I went to a cash machine to withdraw some money, my card was withheld and I discovered that my joint bank account had been frozen. This convinced me all the more of the threat that Neil and my father both posed to my recovery. I went in to the nearest branch of my bank and burst into tears as I tried to explain to the cashier that my card had been swallowed and that I had no means of getting any money. She kindly ushered me into a private room where I explained that I'd just left my husband and that he and my father were trying to prevent me from leaving. After a few phone calls she was able to get authorisation to permit me to withdraw a small amount of money from our joint account.

The same day, I headed in to central London to register with employment agencies. There were a lot of vacancies available at the time so I felt hopeful that it wouldn't take long to get a job. Afterwards I made my way to Hatton Garden to find a jeweller who might be prepared to buy my rings, not knowing if I'd be able to withdraw any more money. I sold the ring my Grandma had left me and this gave me enough to live on for two weeks.

It was a strange feeling settling in to the new environment, but I was running on autopilot and just putting one foot in front of the other. I cleaned the flat as best I could and did a shop for the week. After going for interviews, I was offered two jobs but was scared of the responsibility of one of them so I accepted the other which paid less but seemed a lot less daunting. The people were really friendly at the office and helped me to settle in. I did tell one lady that I'd just left my husband but didn't go into any details.

A couple of weeks after I'd moved into my therapist's flat, I received a letter from Neil. The friend I'd entrusted my new address with had obviously disclosed it to him. In the letter he had accused me of thinking my therapist was a god. He said how worried he'd been when I'd used the words 'he is the truth'. I don't actually remember saying those words, I would probably have said 'he always speaks the truth' but that must have been how it had come across to Neil. His last paragraph closed with the words, 'Think about what you're doing, and why you're staying with that bogus bull-shitter!'

A week after that he turned up with some of my belongings and asked if I'd like to go out to a gig with him. I declined but thanked him and he left after a quick hug.

Six months later Neil called me at work and said he wanted a divorce so that he could move on with his life. Two weeks after that I received a petition for divorce on the grounds of unreasonable behaviour. It described how my regime and food plan was the cause of the breakdown of our marriage due to meal times being out of sync with his and that normal social occasions were often hard to plan for and were inconvenienced by my food restrictions. I didn't contest it and the divorce proceeded. I was more upset that the very thing that had saved my life, my food plan, was being condemned. I took off my rings and reverted to using my maiden name.

Although I was made to leave Neil, I was still allowed occasional contact with my parents for the first couple of years since moving up to London; usually at Christmas and on my birthday. I felt drained and depressed after every visit to them as I felt I had to spend my time defending my recovery programme. My father wanted to know why I had no friends, why I no longer dressed up and whether I'd gone off men. My parents spoke of brainwashing and when I mentioned it to my therapist he said, 'Of course it's brain washing, think about it, that's exactly what you need'. It made complete sense to me given my background.

When my grandfather was dying I saw a lot of my family during the last two weeks of his life. My therapist believed that all older people were deliberately being neglected in hospitals around the country so that they would die and free up beds. And so he told me to intervene. My grandfather had been admitted to Bromley Hospital following a severe kidney infection but then went on to contract *c. difficile* from the hospital. My therapist told me to visit him to persuade him to move into a private hospital. I did talk to him to try to encourage him to go privately but he said he felt he was getting the best care where he was. I was then told to make an appointment with the consultant to discuss what they were planning to do to treat him. I went with my mother but the consultant said it was time to allow him to have morphine so he could let go and slip away. I asked if they would be prepared to give him probiotics to counteract the *c. difficile* infection, but while it's common practise to use probiotics as part of the treatment for such infections today, the consultant looked at me blankly and I was unable to convince him. I went back one last time with my mother to sit with him during his last hours. I had mixed emotions: the holier-than-thou feelings that I'd experienced as a result of my therapist's intervention plan were starting to dissipate and the simple emotion of feeling anguished for my grandfather in his last moments took over.

After the funeral and wake, I drove home feeling sick with myself for the part I'd played of the spiritually superior daughter who had failed at the very least to try to persuade the doctors to try the probiotics. Looking back, it was probably far too late by then. When I got home I climbed into bed, pulled the duvet over my head and went to sleep.

On the instructions of my therapist, I reverted to minimal contact with my parents once again. I believed everything he told me and felt my family didn't care if I lost my recovery as they simply didn't understand why I couldn't just moderate my eating. My therapist had said many times that there were no other effective treatment programmes. This wasn't hard to believe as I had indeed experienced the futile but well-meaning help that had been offered me. I was told that even the traditional anonymous programme for overeaters had become largely a place for people to have 'fat serenity'. The internet was just a baby in those days and therefore I had no knowledge of or access to the effective programmes that were budding in the US at the time; I simply had no choice.

Chapter 10: Svengali

For the next few years I devoted my time outside of work studying for a degree with the Open University. My therapist believed that it was critical for us to keep busy as part of our recovery. During my sixth-form years I had become so debilitated by my food addiction that I had completely loused up my A levels. I spent so many lessons lying on the floor in the school toilets suffering the effects of laxatives or bunking off to get over a sugar or alcohol-fuelled hangover that I had no chance of catching up. And I didn't care.

Once in recovery, however, I surprised myself with how well I did with my assignments. Although my therapist didn't permit me to look at my grades during the course, after the exam was over I discovered my marks were consistently high.

This was ground-breaking for me. The changes that happened in me as a result of my recovery which enabled me to not only eat healthily but to study and complete my degree convinced me even more that I was doing the right thing. I had become a functioning human being; no longer an emotional foetus wrapped in an adult's body.

It wasn't just in my studies that I was doing well either. By this time I'd moved on from the first job I'd taken when I moved up to London and was now working for an investment bank in the marketing department. My end of year appraisals were outstanding and I could hardly believe they were written about me. I thought of Du Maurier's Trilby, and wondered whether my therapist's spell might one day shatter along with my newly found abilities.

I was completely and utterly dependent on him. I started to worry about his well-being—not from any compassion on my part—but from an intense fear that if anything should happen to him it would be the end of me.

Every night all of his clients would have an allocated time to call him to report their respective food plans for the following day. If, on the rare occasion he didn't answer the phone or call me, I would start to become frantic. After thirty minutes or so of no contact and having tried all of his phone numbers I would start to call around hospitals to make sure he hadn't been admitted. I would be distraught by this stage imagining all sorts of accidents. When he finally did call, I would almost sob with relief that he was fine and therefore I would be too.

My therapist slowly and steadily took control over every part of my life, even over the most trivial decisions, such as the colours I was allowed to paint the kitchen and lounge walls. He kept putting up his fees and insisting that this was a socialist system of payment. All of his clients had to pay as much as they could possibly afford so that those less well-off could receive his help too.

He would often say that his life was devoted to rescuing us from our condition of spiritual and moral bankruptcy. It was the basis of truth that made everything he said so compelling. He made no bones about the measures he had to go to fix our heads. He once said to me, roaring with laughter, that one of his clients had shouted, 'Stop it! You're raping my psyche!'

I laughed along wanting him to think well of me for finding humour in what seemed so brutal but so necessary.

In one of my therapy sessions I remember saying to him that I felt like piggy-in-the-middle; meaning between him and my parents. But when I saw a look of such rage on his face—something I'd never seen before—I quickly asserted that I meant that I felt torn between my mother and father. His reaction had scared me and I was desperate not to offend him in case he pulled the plug on my recovery. From then on I was careful to censor everything I said in case it would enrage him again.

Despite feeling that my freedom was being taken from me bit by bit, I still felt unique and part of the chosen few.

But I swung from feeling floaty and spiritual to feeling very low and despondent, particularly when I got up each morning. But I accepted the pain as both part of what my therapist would call the healing process and of the philosophy of surrender and suffering that he espoused.

We were given prayers on slips of paper to learn off-by-heart to reinforce his beliefs about how we have to suffer and die to self here on earth in order to be truly at peace. The Confederate's Prayer[4], as it's known, helped to hammer the message home:

> *I asked God for strength, that I might achieve;*
> *I was made weak, that I might learn humbly to obey.*
> *I asked for health, that I might do greater things;*
> *I was given infirmity, that I might do better things.*
> *I asked for riches, that I might be happy;*
> *I was given poverty, that I might be wise.*
> *I asked for power, that I might have the praise of men;*
> *I was given weakness, that I might feel the need of God.*
> *I asked for all things, that I might enjoy life;*
> *I was given life, that I might enjoy all things.*
> *I got nothing that I asked for, but everything I hoped for.*
> *Almost despite myself, my unspoken prayers were answered.*
> *I am among all men most richly blessed.*

In addition to the prayers, my therapist gave us some audio cassettes and later CDs of Christian music. He would say that while he had to be tough on us, we could feel comforted by listening to spiritual songs. I listened to them over and over again, every day for years and years. They were very emotional and helped make me feel set-apart and spiritual. Lyrics included words along the lines of: *Can a mother forget her little child? Maybe she can.* And the one he insisted on us listening to the most, *I am willing God, to be exactly what you want me to be.*

The majority of the songs were about self-sacrifice, accepting God's will and of being God's most precious and beloved children. It helped to fix in my mind that my therapist's will was God's will and reinforced what he was telling me about how my parents had been unable to give me the love that I needed to nurture me and help me develop into a well-rounded individual.

My therapy sessions were down to one a week by this stage but I continued to speak to him on the phone every day to commit my food plan. I never forgot his words that I would be married again by the time I was 28, though, and this thought, together with my studies and my work, kept me going.

Chapter 11: Shelley

A couple of years after I'd moved into the flat, another client moved in too. This was quite a surprise to me given that I was forbidden to speak to any of the other clients he had. Shelley was suffering from a severe emotional crisis after having seen several other therapists who focused on trying to force out painful childhood memories. The methods used to extract memories have been described as at best traumatising and at worst as causing false memory syndrome.

Shelley would talk about getting her memory back about sexual abuse she believed she experienced once from a relative. Whether real or misremembered she was deeply traumatised. In all likelihood our brains blot out painful memories for good reason. Shelley's previous therapist believed you needed to 'lance the boil' before recovery was possible. She pushed and pushed her to come up with painful memories, even encouraging her to use art as therapy to draw from her imagination and then interpret the images.

Shelley had come into therapy as she was trying to quit using Valium to help with her depression.

Our therapist also believed that Shelley's depression was rooted in pain from the past and that only by digging it out would she be able to recover.

Shelley moved into the once padlocked spare room in the basement and shared the flat with me for just over three years. She was funny, really funny and we became good friends. We'd often prepare our meals together in the evening and she'd have me in fits, shrieking with laughter.

She was resourceful too. Shelley managed to wangle a skip out of Hackney Council which meant we could clear all the rubble out of the garden and plant some flowers and a beautifully scented Honeysuckle bush. It became somewhere I loved to sit out in, especially on warm summer evenings and I put up bird and squirrel feeders. Shelly loved our therapist, he'd dramatically changed her life too and she was no longer on anti-depressants. We both felt we'd been on the brink of suicide before we met him.

We spent hours in conversation about our childhoods and I remember feeling an irrational jealousy about how much worse hers had been compared to mine. Shelley often said she thought that I must have been abused but try as I might I remembered nothing. I even tried the art therapy on her suggestion—still nothing. I felt like a fraud at times to have had such a normal childhood in comparison yet had still gone on to suffer from mental illness.

Shelley had several health practitioners and I remember her waving a battery-powered hand-held gadget over her food as this would apparently neutralise negative energy from her meal. The machine looked very home-made and I'm sure if you opened it, it would have been empty apart from a battery and a connection to a small red light bulb. She was paying her practitioners a fortune and they had convinced her that she had a 'pre-cancerous' condition and that it was caused by an overgrowth of candida in her gut. Finally she was diagnosed with myalgic encephalomyelitis (ME). She certainly had very low energy levels and I'm sure she wasn't faking it. But she was vulnerable, just like I was, to those who offered help and then took advantage.

The time came when Shelley and our therapist had a disagreement. He told me that she was arrogant and full of self-pity and that he didn't like her and wanted to make her feel so unwelcome that she would vacate the flat. To engineer this he told me to avoid eye contact with her and no longer smile or chat to her. He told me to unscrew the padlock on the remaining locked room and to use it as my bedroom. I'd been sleeping in the lounge on the sofa up until that point. He explained that she had asked him if she could have the upstairs room instead of the tiny basement room she was in and so by giving it to me he believed it would have the effect of making her feel snubbed. It felt so unkind to do that and to suddenly blank her after how close we had become.

Shelley asked me what was wrong and my therapist had told me to say that as part of my recovery I was to learn to stop engaging in what he called compulsive talking. She didn't tell me what had happened between them but said she'd been feeling so desperate that she'd called the Samaritans. When I told my therapist, he said that due to her arrogance he had told her to get lost and stopped her therapy but said she could remain in the flat. In the end, however, he forced her out by making me tell her that her room was needed by someone else and that she had three weeks to vacate.

When Shelley moved out, my therapist insisted that I must have no more contact with her. Apart from a letter that was confiscated and therefore I never got to read, it was the last I heard of her for a few years.

The almost adoration of my therapist that I had felt since I started the programme had gone sour but the fear of him remained. I was desperate not to be kicked out in the same way as Shelley had been. I had no doubts that I wouldn't be able to survive without him. The basement room was once again padlocked.

Chapter 12: For the Greater Good

Over the years I learned a few things about my therapist's background. He had grown up in Singapore and Malaysia and had had a strict Catholic upbringing. His mother had physically and emotionally abused him as a child. She regularly beat him and would then do penance for her sins by sprinkling rice on the floor and kneeling on it to 'mortify her flesh'. Other than this he spoke very little about his past except to say he had rejected being a practising Catholic.

My therapist came to England in the 70s as a teacher and had to put up with racism and prejudice. How he became a therapist and whether he was qualified I have no idea. His business card said BA and I'm pretty sure he had a degree in philosophy and education but whether he was qualified in psychology or certified as a therapist I couldn't say. In fact he rejected pretty much all of the notions of traditional psychology: from self-esteem issues to a complete dismissal of the idea of genetically determined personality types. In terms of psychotherapy he believed the traditional notion of the mother as the root cause of all of a person's problems. It's not a very big leap to see the connections between his mother's treatment of him, his Catholic upbringing and why he was to cause my own mother so much pain and grief.

My therapist told me he had 48 clients in his care at this stage and I always wondered how there were enough hours in the day to deal with everyone. He seemed to have a photographic memory and could recall everything you told him. He had the ability to make you feel like you were the only client he had.

He told me how he had to separate his clients from their families because of the risk to their recovery. Many of those with children were told to leave them behind. Several of the women were also told to leave their homes to live in various dwellings that were in his name or associated with him somehow—be they flats, caravans or bedsits. He didn't need a lock and key for us, the psychological bonds that he held us with were far stronger. The fact that he kept caged birds started to feel rather fitting too.

For him, the ultimate good justified doing almost anything. He believed that with the cunning, deceitful, arrogant and self-pitying addicts in his care, he was justified in meting out the most extreme and psychologically brutal measures in the name of abstinence. He often said our egos were so severely inflated that they needed to be bludgeoned to death. What made his theories so compelling, however, were the truths that underpinned them and of course the astoundingly effective food plan.

He once said to me, 'Always remember this Candace, I have to be ruthless with you because we're dealing with a killer illness. I love you but won't always be able to say so as it's my job to keep one step ahead of your disease'.

* * *

A few weeks after Shelley moved out, my therapist announced that he would occasionally need to stay the night. I would wake up suddenly at the sound of his key in the latch and even though I knew it was him it would always make me sit bolt upright with my heart pounding. He would trudge downstairs and unlock the padlock of the basement room. As my room was directly above his, I could hear him on the phone taking his other clients' food plans for the next day or yelling and screaming at them for some transgression or other. I'd try not to hear what he was saying but I remember feeling relieved that I wasn't on the receiving end of his tirades.

When he finally fell asleep, his snoring was deafening. He would be gone by the time I got up leaving the basin full of pubic hair and a large puddle of urine on the floor around the toilet. One of my cats, Esme, had the most unpleasant habit of rolling ecstatically in his pee and the smell would linger for days no matter how much I tried to clean her fur.

Chapter 13: Shame and Punishment

It was in 1994, six months after Shelley had left, that I did something that would dramatically change how my therapist treated me. I continued to think about his promise that I would be married again by the time I was 28 and when that birthday had come and gone I decided to mention it. It was like a slap in the face when he dismissed it completely and said that relationships were out of the question for the heterosexual clients he saw. Had I been a lesbian, however, he told me he would have helped me to find a partner. As for men, he believed the overwhelming majority were too shallow and into appearances for me to maintain my recovery if I was in a relationship. I felt angry and cheated but kept it to myself.

Not long after the conversation there was a killing spree of cats in the neighbourhood. I started to investigate what was happening as I was fearful for my own animals and hated to see cherished pets lying in the street with their necks broken. I did a leaflet drop around the block to find out if anyone was letting their dog out alone.

One of my neighbours from a few streets away, Mike, came by to let me know that his Burmese cat had been killed. With minimal interest shown by the RSPCA, Mike and I started working together to investigate the killings by speaking to other pet owners.

I had been instantly attracted to Mike but felt completely safe in my frumpy clothes and kept the conversation to spiritual matters. I thought I could sense a tension between us every time we passed each other but knowing he was married I didn't for one moment think that anything would come of it.

We went out night after night walking around the neighbourhood to try to discover where the dog might live. We had a map with markers showing the locations that dead cats had been discovered and were able to narrow down the most likely roads that the dog might be living in. I put up some posters urging people to contact us with any information and finally a photographer called me with hard evidence: he'd captured a picture of the dog on camera with a dead cat in his mouth.

From the photograph, we both recognised a dog that we'd seen in the street while we were interviewing people in the neighbourhood. We sat in Mike's car that night to 'stake out' the dog's home. Sure enough, in the early hours of the morning his owners opened the front door and let the dog out on its own. With the photographic evidence and the address of the suspect dog the RSPCA stepped in and prosecuted the owners. Darky, as the dog was known, was rehomed.

Mike then suggested that we should go out to celebrate and I agreed. He started to probe into my background and told me I shouldn't hide myself away so much. He started to criticise my reclusive lifestyle and although I disliked the questioning at the same time I liked the attention and I still felt safely protected by my ugly clothes.

When we got back, he walked me to my door. I felt his breath on my neck and in a split-second his hands were all over me. The sudden and unexpected pleasure made me gasp. I had had no physical human contact of any description for eight years and it was intoxicating. But what was to follow was a sordid affair which made me feel sick to the core with self-hatred and hatred for Mike. We indulged in snatched liaisons at his friend's empty house and waking up next to him in the mornings, he would swear at me and turn over. I would grab my clothes and get a cab home feeling used and despised. After a pregnancy scare and feeling utterly wretched I told him we couldn't see each other again.

A few months after the liaisons were over and overwhelmed with feelings of guilt as well as fear for my recovery I confessed to my therapist. I wrote everything down in a letter and left it on the desk for him in the front room. By this stage, my therapist was holding therapy sessions in the flat every Sunday to save on the cost of office space. He saw two clients, one after the other, before me so I was confined to my bedroom for the duration. The other client would wait in the kitchen—the only other spare room available.

I sat on my bed waiting for my session, feeling sick and desperate. His voice grew louder as he opened the door to let the last client out of the lounge and into the hallway. I stood up, my heart thumping as if it was in my throat. It was my turn. I walked in looking at the floor and sat down on the old, broken sofa.

He was silent for what seemed like ages. Then he spoke, his voice trembling with carefully contained rage, 'I'm in shock Candace. No one has ever behaved like you and survived to tell the tale. Other clients who messed around like that have lost their abstinence and are now dead. I'm not sure you'll survive this'.

I couldn't look at him, my face burned with shame and my heart continued to thump violently as his words sank in. He paused again and then suddenly exploded, 'HOW DARE YOU TREAT ME LIKE THAT AFTER ALL I'VE DONE FOR YOU! THE OTHERS TREAT ME WITH ABSOLUTE OBEDIENCE, RESPECT AND GRATITUDE.'

'I'm so sorry' I said over and over. I fully expected him to banish me. Then a wave of relief surged through me as he told me that the only possible way to save my life was to completely and utterly destroy my monumental ego. That meant there was some hope that I wasn't going to be banished, just punished. I was beside myself with the fear of losing my abstinence and going back to the hell of my former life. I was ready to do whatever he told me just as long as I could stay in recovery and not be kicked out by him.

I sat and listened as he handed out my sentence; hoping it wouldn't be too extreme but steeling myself for anything. First of all I had to sever all connections with my family apart from a note I was to send to my mother once a month to say I was 'alive and well'. I was no longer allowed to make eye contact with anyone unless it was at work and I was specifically discussing instructions. I was forbidden to smile and was forced to slow down my speech so that I would sound simple. I was told to go out the next morning and buy a copy of the Pink Paper and take it to work with me every day so that people would assume I was gay. I was no longer allowed to read my post and had to hand all of it to him still sealed. Internet (other than purely work related), television, radio and magazines were forbidden.

I wrote down my instructions while he continued sentencing me. He told me that my appearance would have to become more extreme and that I would have to put on a stone in weight. I discovered later that the 'surrender weight' he had told me I was to weigh was a lie and that I actually weighed far more than that. I was forbidden to use a mirror or remove facial hair and deal with spots. I wasn't to touch my face but was allowed to use a flannel to wash it.

The next part of my punishment involved leaving voicemail messages on his phones every day, rather like writing lines. He had several mobile numbers but each one could only accommodate between 30 and 50 voicemails at a time. This meant I had to buy him an extra six mobile phone contracts in order to accommodate the hundreds of voicemails I had to leave him. Some of the messages were short, such as 'No smiling or talking at work' and some were what he called 'sick' thoughts. I had to be on constant vigil about the thoughts I was having throughout the day and as soon as I caught a negative thought about another person or my appearance I was to record a voicemail on one of his phones. A third variety involved learning off by heart and reciting large passages from Thomas a Kempis' *The Imitation of Christ*—a code for living written for monks c. 1427. It started with about 200 voicemails a day and increased to 2,000 a day over the next 16 years. My final tally of mobile phones was 20 and my monthly mobile bills came to over £500.

My therapist then went on to give me a financial penalty with three quarters of my income to be paid to him from that point on. I also had to sever any emotional connections with objects my parents had given me and was told I must drop them all off at the charity shop the next day. I found it heart rending to have to take gifts and treasured soft toys to leave at the Oxfam shop and was quite devastated when I had to give up my favourite cuddly toy, a large, huggable

Steiff® pig named Paris that my father had bought me when we went on a trip to France. This pig brought back memories not only of my father but of my little brother who I loved dearly and was a source of pure joy and light during an otherwise rather dark childhood and adolescence. He and I would play hunt-the-pig when we were children and so giving it up was like cutting the final, fragile strand that connected us.

I was told I had come within a hair's breadth of losing my recovery which for an addict is tantamount to risking death from suicide or overdose. I was deeply ashamed of my behaviour and felt that punishment was justified. Why it meant a total severance of contact from my family was never very clear although he blamed my parents for my addiction and said that as a result they would undermine my recovery and lead me back into active disease.

Finally, after two hours of sentencing me, he got up to leave and then turned back to throw a few crumbs my way, 'I still love you, you know'.

As the front door closed, I sat frozen on the sofa. I was sick with fear and anxiety for my recovery and desperately sad at the same time. It was like the gates had clanged shut on my ever having contact with my family again or indeed ever having a semblance of a normal life with a family of my own. The thing that saved my sanity over the years was probably some genetically-determined ability to suck up the pain and keep going.

Chapter 14: Full on Purgatory

At the time of my confession I was working a night shift at an American legal firm to earn more money for my therapist. At work the next evening I wore my hair scraped back in a bun and had my newly acquired extreme clothes on. I put a copy of the Pink Paper on my desk, as instructed, but folded it over to hide a picture of a man's crotch. My usual smile was replaced with an anguished look and a deep frown. I couldn't look anyone in the eye I was so ashamed of my appearance.

People must have noticed something had changed but no one said anything apart from a muttered comment from a colleague about my having had charisma-bypass surgery. I worked on my own through that night and had my therapist's words ringing in my ears constantly. I was distraught, disturbed and didn't want to live but didn't want to take my own life either. In my mind my thoughts slammed against each other as I felt dirty and disgusting about the affair. My therapist had insisted I write about it in minute detail for him to read and so I did this even to the point of describing anatomical dimensions. His eyes had flashed with rage as he spat my words back at me.

My head felt so messed up that I was scared rigid and breathing rapidly. I thought I was on the brink of a nervous breakdown and when I told my therapist he said that a breakdown was a personal choice, not something that would just happen to me. That comforted me somewhat.

On my next therapy session he pronounced that I was gay and that the affair was me trying to prove I wasn't. There was more confusion as I tried to work it out in my mind. Then a wave of depression hit me at the thought of being forced into a relationship with a woman. He looked at me, eyes glinting as he tried to suppress his laughter, held an imaginary gun to his head and pulled the trigger.

My mind seethed for days as I tried to cope with all my emotions and then a week later he announced I wasn't gay. 'More's the pity' he said gloating 'I would have helped find you a partner, I know a woman who looks just like Winston Churchill'.

Why did I put up with it all? I simply felt that I had no choice, that no-one else out there had the knowledge about the food plan. I knew the food plan on its own wasn't enough, that I needed someone to be accountable to. He would have kicked me out if I'd protested in any way and the thought of going back to a life of bulimia would mean a short trip back to hell. I have no doubts I would take my life if that were the case.

Over the next few months, my punishments were refined and increased as I left messages on his voicemails and described my thoughts and behaviour. I was forbidden to have my hair cut and I would wind it into a huge bun or wear a plait. On leaving the house I had to wear a headscarf and walk with my head bowed, looking at the pavement a metre or so in front of me. All my clothes were either home-made or the ugliest things I could find at charity shops.

I made myself some long skirts with elasticated waists in drab olive and brown and found a particularly hideous acrylic cardigan with a pink and white diamond pattern on it. I swapped my glasses for a pair of old-fashioned, men's steel-rimmed glasses. I wore men's socks (although at work I swapped them for woolly tights) and Mrs Doubtfire-style brown, lace-up shoes. I wheeled a tartan shopping trolley around with me to complete the picture.

My wardrobe was to stay the same regardless of the season and I was told it was especially good for me to boil on a hot day. In summer on the stifling Piccadilly Line tube I would be dressed in my thick jumpers, long skirt, headscarf and a heavy coat on top. The sweat poured off me, running down my tummy and down the backs of my legs, making splash marks on the floor.

The opted-out clothes were supposed to stop me from obsessing about my appearance, in addition to putting men off me, but I felt ashamed and ugly. I didn't worry when I was out and about shopping anonymously but at work I was embarrassed about my appearance and resented other women who were able to dress well. The expression, 'Dress like a pig, get treated like a pig' was mentioned to me on several occasions. It felt like a blow to the chest but I swallowed the feelings each time. I developed a kind of 'jolly fat person' bravado and scorned people I considered vain.

I was told to get rid of my car and bicycle which I believe was to limit my freedom and mobility. I was to live rather like the Amish so that anything that might contribute to pride or vanity would be rejected. My washing machine and laptop were my two remaining luxuries.

At work, when I confessed to feeling attracted to one of the lawyers, my therapist devised another extreme measure to make me even more unattractive. From my next meal, and all my meals thereafter I was told to eat a whole bulb of raw garlic (yes bulb, not just a single clove) as part of my vegetable portion. The garlic burned my tongue, mouth and oesophagus and gave me terrible stomach pains and nausea. When I reported this to my therapist he was furious but finally relented and allowed me to cook the garlic. Still, I must have absolutely reeked.

When I confessed to pulling out a hair from my face one evening he was furious and told me to get some cotton gloves to wear at home and that at night I should bind my hands with bandages so that I didn't have the excuse to touch my face while half asleep. I told him how upset I was about having to walk around with two inch long chin hairs so he threatened me with having to glue on a theatrical beard every day and that was enough to stop me mentioning them again. And while I never brought the subject up again I was deeply distressed to have to walk around with whiskers on my face. I remember sitting at a bus stop in Dalston and touching the hairs with my fingers, they felt like pubic hairs and I wanted to wrench them all out. Somehow it was okay for other women to have facial hair if they didn't mind, but I felt desperately ugly and wished I could wear a niqab to hide my face.

That night I put on my cotton gloves, flannel nightie and used a bandage to bind my fingers on one hand and used my teeth to help secure it on the other. Jake, one of my neighbour's cats, climbed under the duvet and snuggled up with me. With his faintly fishy breath, deep purr and warm, fat body he was enormously comforting.

The small respite wasn't to last though and I woke with a start to the doorbell and staggered downstairs to answer it. The communal door was open as decorators were painting at the front of the property. I undid the latch and asked who was there.

'CANDACE! LONG TIME NO SEE!' His voice boomed and I wondered if he wanted the men painting the windows in the front to hear. It was Mike. I felt my body seize up and I couldn't breathe. I'm not sure exactly what he said but I was standing there in my old-fashioned nightie, bandages and a pair of mens' socks. I hung my head, hardly able to comprehend the reality of the situation. He'd moved away from the area and I thought I'd never see him again. He was the symbol of my shame, guilt and immorality and the reason my hopes for the future had been dashed.

On a very superficial level, I simply didn't want to look up and for him to see my facial hair and spots. I muttered something about working nights and he must have seen the anguish in my face. 'SHOCK, HORROR CANDACE!'.

He sounded very offended but I just kept muttering about being half asleep. He left still shouting 'SHOCK, HORROR' over and over, possibly for the benefit of the decorators and to save his pride. I climbed back into bed, curled into a ball of shame and pulled the covers over my head. That was the last I saw of Mike.

* * *

In the weeks that followed I had to do what's known in 12-step programmes as my Step Four: a '...fearless moral inventory'[5] of my life to date. I wrote countless pages outlining all of my defects of character and moral flaws throughout my life, my resentments, my relationships and mistreatment of others.

This, however, was the first really useful exercise I had done in the seven years since I had been under my therapist's control. In recovery programmes this vital step enables addicts to see their faults in full colour. This is essential for both the critical acceptance of powerlessness over addiction and for keeping alive the memories of the depths to which addicts can sink when using. It helps to spur the daily recovery practises necessary to prevent addicts from picking up their drug of choice to blot out their feelings.

In 12-step programmes for abstinence from alcohol, those who've given up drink but haven't dealt with their emotional demons are called dry-drunks. This is considered to be a dangerous space to be in. It's only the beginning of recovery to put the cork in the bottle or put down the equivalent substance of choice. Take away the anaesthesia and acute and painful feelings flood in and can be overwhelming.

I had been just like that for the first seven years under my therapist's control. He had kept the focus on my family background which had stirred up painful emotions and built up resentment towards my parents as the cause of my disease. Though the pseudo spirituality held my feelings in check somewhat, when my emotional instability reared its ugly head I was prone to irrational outbursts of tears or anger and often felt very down. At work I would storm off in an angry strop if anyone hinted at my work being less than perfect and while the liaisons with Mike were going on I was completely obsessed with him in a way which led to my life becoming unmanageable again.

In fact being in love or infatuated is very similar to taking drugs with the craving, obsession, withdrawal and guilt it entails. I would stand at the window to see when his car would pull in, or sit by the phone waiting for him to call me. Mike had been 'camping out' in my head and I was exhausted both mentally and physically. I would sleep to blot out my feelings and on one occasion when I had a nap in the evening I woke up so late I nearly missed my last meal. As for the sex, I felt nothing. But being desired and having physical contact gave me a hit. The whole affair and nearly missing a meal really frightened me. Skipping meals is a strong relapse warning sign and if I didn't correct my actions I knew I would be off down a slippery slope.

The step-four inventory I carried out was the first time I had come face-to-face with my character flaws. I'd often seen myself as a victim, particularly with all the focus on my poor parents being the culprits. Writing all about my life, however, I could see for the first time how my disease hadn't just affected me but all the people I'd come into contact with. I had become a user of people just as much and sometimes more than they had used me.

So, while it was a necessary, indeed critical, measure to do the inventory and should have been done after the first few months of stabilising on the food plan, its purpose was never intended to give counsellors or sponsors a weapon to continually judge, beat and condemn those in their care. But this is exactly what it had become.

It wasn't the last I'd heard from my therapist about the affair either. A while later he was describing some women who had helped him up the stairs with his suitcase. His eyes were glistening with tears as he said how lovely women were but then he must have caught my hopeful expression:

'Not YOU for Christ's sake! You're like a bitch on heat... more like a man... a sexual predator'.

Chapter 15: Never Good Enough

Ever since my confession and moral inventory, my therapist had changed his attitude to me completely. At around the same time he was diagnosed with Type II diabetes though he must have had it for years. His moods became darker and darker.

He told me in no uncertain terms that I was the most arrogant and despicable person he'd ever met because of what I had done and that this was especially so because I was in recovery rather than a practising addict who didn't have the necessary information to get well. I thought back with shame at how he had once said I was one of the loveliest people he'd met. Gone was the look of caring in his eyes and instead I saw pure hatred. He seemed to relish any moment he could in attacking and criticising me and controlling absolutely everything about my life. He even dictated the type of underwear and sanitary protection I was allowed to use. I had to cover the mirrored tiles in the bathroom and throw away all other mirrors and anything that could be used as a mirror and was banned from ever looking at my reflection again. I didn't see myself in a mirror for the next 15 years.

I took on board everything he told me and tried so hard to please him and make up for my behaviour by doing everything I was told to the point of perfection. I would sit with my head bowed at my therapy sessions waiting for my instructions for the week ahead. He would sit looking at me with hatred in his eyes and if I dared to protest or question him, he would slam his fist down on the desk, thundering 'YOU CAN JUST GET LOST, CANDACE, WHO THE HELL ARE YOU TO QUESTION ME... YOU WHO ARE MENTALLY ILL!'

I was particularly upset about my more extreme appearance. It wasn't fun to meet people for the first time and watch their jaws drop and their faces redden. But on another level I tried to view it as an interesting experiment in psycho-social interactions to see how people responded to my physical appearance. Shop keepers and staff reacted to me in the most extreme way as they seemed to assume I wanted to steal from them. I was challenged on numerous occasions and even though obviously innocent they were still rude, 'You look wrong so you must be guilty', they seemed to be saying. I was routinely shouted at in the street and on buses for some reason too.

I bumped into my sister-in-law one evening as I was going in to work. Her eyes widened in alarm and she stood there with her mouth open staring at me unable to speak. I asked how everyone was but she didn't seem to be able to compose herself enough to form her words and didn't know where to look so we soon went our separate ways. I remember what I was wearing, my olive green skirt with an old coat and an old fashioned scarf on my head (worn like a 1940s housewife), thick tights and my brown lace up shoes. It must have been such a contrast from when she had last seen me.

At the care homes I went to as part of my voluntary work, staff had the same reaction to me and when I reported the neglect I saw with one lady I used to visit—faeces up her fingernails and having to sit in stinking, wet pads for hours—they tried to lodge a formal complaint against me with the charity I volunteered for.

The number of men who would either try to grope me, expose themselves to me or kerb crawl was ridiculous. I remember sitting in a shelter at Stoke Newington station eating my lunch while waiting for the train. A man walked up and squatted next to me. I ignored him completely while he pleasured himself, reached his finale and walked away. I felt offended but more than anything sad when I thought of all the vulnerable people with learning difficulties who are abused and exploited throughout their lives.

My therapist said that the more verbal attacks I received the better it was for me to deal with my vanity. Far worse than putting up with people's insults, however, was the part of my penance that banned social interaction. Not smiling or making eye contact at work felt so rude and anti-social, particularly when someone smiled at me and asked how I was. I swung from doing as I was told—looking away and mumbling at people—to smiling and chatting. My therapist told me that only complete honesty would save me, so every time I broke the rules I confessed and had to face the consequences. Usually it would mean I would have to leave an extra few hundred messages a day on his phones. On other occasions the penalties were far more distressful.

One particular time after I'd confessed to chatting at work, he threatened me by saying he would force me to have my cats euthanized if I did it again. This led to an episode of (what I later realised) was hyperventilation which in turn led me to collapse at work. I was sent to hospital and the triage nurses assessed me as potentially having suffered a stroke.

My therapist called the hospital as I'd left him a message to say what had happened. They put him through to me while I was waiting to be seen by the doctor and he asked me who I had put down as my next of kin. I told him that the hospital files had my mother's name recorded and he insisted I change it to his name. 'If you're about to meet your maker' he joked unkindly 'the last thing you want is to have your parents turn up'.

I was certain that I was dying as I was also waiting to hear the results of a brain MRI that had been carried out due to various neurological symptoms I had been experiencing. My heart was pounding as I waited for the doctor to examine me. They could find nothing wrong and though I mentioned the MRI they said that I should go home and wait to see the neurologist. I then realised that I must have been over-breathing because of the distress of being faced with having to have the cats put to sleep though I didn't tell the hospital staff. I was offered psychological counselling but I turned it down and left feeling ashamed.

Another time I had to confess about talking at work was while I was working a graveyard shift at another invest-ment bank in the city. Again I had changed jobs to earn more money when my therapist's fees continued to soar. I worked on my own through the night and poured everything I had into my work. Many of the bankers were there well into the small hours and were always friendly and appreciated my work. One evening an intern offered me some grapes and, not wanting to offend, I thanked him and put them in my bag to take home and got on with my project. When I spoke to my therapist that night I told him about the exchange but could not have anticipated the rage he flew into. He ranted and screamed at me for having talked to a man at work. I was standing at a call box in Liverpool Street Station at the time (as I wasn't allowed to take my mobile phones out of the house with me) and broke down crying as he tore into me; it was a feeling I can only describe as like having my throat ripped out by a pit bull. A man wandering past asked if I was okay and I put on a brave smile and mouthed, 'Fine, thank you.'

My therapist continued the attack and whether he'd just heard or wanted to create an impact on me he chose this time to tell me that he'd heard that Shelley had killed herself after two unsuccessful previous attempts. All I could hear was my long drawn out gasp as I took in what he'd just said. I sobbed hysterically. I was devastated to hear what she'd done and at the same time was paralysed with fear that if my therapist got rid of me too, then I would also end up committing suicide.

Chapter 16: Trying to Teach

After the trauma of hearing what Shelly had done, I buried myself in my studies. The embargo on all news, radio, television and internet (other than for work purposes) left two things for me to read: my course work and The Imitation of Christ which, according to my therapist, was the perfect blueprint for us to live by. It championed a life of obedience, self-sacrifice, solitude and prayer:

'IT IS a very great thing to obey; to live under a superior and not to be one's own master, for it is much safer to be subject than it is to command. Many live in obedience more from necessity than from love. Such become discontented and dejected on the slightest pretext; they will never gain peace of mind unless they subject themselves wholeheartedly for the love of God.

Go where you may, you will find no rest except in humble obedience to the rule of authority.' [6]

I remembered with sadness how Shelley referred to the author as Thomas 'Laughing Boy' Kempis and how I missed her irreverence.

I had to learn large chunks of *The Imitation* off by heart and would recall them in my mind and of course leave passages on voicemail for my therapist to check. I was trying so hard to become the spiritual person that the pages insisted on but I didn't experience a calling of any type. I would pray asking to be willing to be transformed, but it always felt like I was praying to a dark void. Despite reading about the virtues of living the life of a religious, I just couldn't shake the underlying yearning for love, physical contact and a family of my own.

As for my coursework, I was surprised that I was allowed to continue with my teacher-training qualification. My therapist had previously decided that it would be a good idea for me to train to be a teacher and so I had signed up for a PGCE course which I studied for in between working nights. My confession and subsequent punishment came just as I was starting the course and I was sure he would make me stop. However, I was to keep on with the course and soon it was time to go in to schools for the practical part of my teacher training.

My clothes were so extreme that I looked like an extra from *Fiddler on the Roof* and my mentor treated me as if I had learning difficulties. When she introduced me to others

she would say in an exaggeratedly slow and clearly enunci-
ated voice, 'This is Candace...she's ok when you get to know
her'. She scoffed at me for coming in early to prepare and if
I did anything 'wrong' while I was training she would shout
at me in front of the children. In an instant I was a school
girl again, feeling stupid and incapable. Fortunately I
changed classes for my next practical training which was in
the same school. My new mentor was wonderful, she didn't
in any way react to my appearance and was down-to-earth
and helpful and asked me to get to school an hour in advance
to prepare. It was such a relief.

Against the odds I passed my PGCE. When I discussed
applying for positions at schools with my therapist he asked
how much I would be earning and then decided that I should
only work as a teacher for one day a week. That way I could
keep the night shift at the investment bank and maintain my
payments to him as well as top them up with the money I
would earn as a supply teacher.

The first teaching job I got was at an Under Fives centre near Finsbury Park. I had only experienced teaching children in reception classes and above so the nursery environment was very new to me. I loved working with the children,
reading to them and thinking up play experiences that they
might enjoy. I loved carrying the very small ones around on
my hip and I didn't mind changing their nappies. It was the
closest thing to having my own children.

While my extreme appearance didn't faze the children, the teachers were somewhat unnerved. When I was busy cleaning the children's toilets one day I heard one teacher say, 'Candace looks so awful, her clothes are hideous!' and her colleague replied, 'She does look awful but I think she might be quite intelligent.' Ever concerned about how I came across, if I couldn't look attractive I was secretly pleased that they might have thought I was intelligent.

There was one incident that is still painful to recall today, however. We were tidying up ready for circle time and two small children were lying on their tummies. I tapped each one in turn on the bottom and said,

'Sit on your bottom it's time for a story'. A member of staff rushed over to me screaming, 'What are you doing? That's such bad practice!' I felt so ashamed and I wanted to run to the toilet to hide. I didn't ask her to clarify if she meant it was the thin end of the wedge of physical abuse or whether she thought it inappropriate to tap two-year-olds on the bottom but either way, in that one moment, I felt overwhelmed with shame. I felt ugly, ridiculous and despised. I had neither the understanding of how to process my emotions in a rational way nor the realisation that perhaps they were triggered by similar feelings from the past. When I got home I was able to have a good cry, but the shame lingered. When I told my therapist he said it was a good thing for me to be attacked by others and reminded me of the line from Thomas à Kempis:

For love of God you should undergo all things cheerfully, all [...] injuries, slanders, rebukes, humiliations, confusions, corrections, and contempt. For these are helps to virtue. These are the trials of Christ's recruit. These form the heavenly crown.[7]

For my next assignment I was in a reception class in a school near Dulwich. I went in every Friday to cover while the main class teacher took the day off to study. I was starting to enjoy the work, got to know and love the children and found the teachers to be helpful and supportive. There was really only one incident where I felt ashamed again. It was when a mother backed me into a corner of the classroom with a jabbing finger and shouted at me for drawing a smiley face on her son's thumb to reward him for good behaviour (something I'd copied from the main class teacher). I was able to bury the feeling though and I soon moved on.

When the contract came up for renewal for the next term and I wasn't rehired I felt the rejection keenly but sucked up the pain and was instructed by my therapist to take some day bookings at schools all around East London. It wasn't easy to do ad hoc supply teaching as a newly qualified teacher; even experienced teachers often have a tough time of it and end up policing the class more than teaching. I was pretty hopeless at crowd control and a fair number of the children had emotional difficulties which made maintaining order very tough.

I remember one booking in Walthamstow where I simply couldn't control a boy who seemed to be insistent on interrupting everything I said and kept charging around the classroom at top speed. At my wit's end I panicked, took his hand and all but dragged him through to another class for help. The teacher watched me pulling him along, gasped and ran up to us scooping him up in her arms and saying, 'It's okay, it's okay, everything's fine'.

I found out later that he was having a terrible time at home. I hated myself for being unable to cope but was at the end of my tether and didn't know what else to do. I returned to the class feeling hopeless and useless and set some independent work for some groups of children while I tried to sit and help the focus group with their maths questions. The noise levels grew and the same teacher burst through the door asking what was going on. I felt more shame as she reprimanded all the children and got them to work quietly. She may as well have shouted at me and sat me in the corner.

During my time as a supply teacher, for some reason a number of children chose to tell me they were being physically abused by relatives. I remember one boy of about six showing me bruises on his arm and another boy of about the same age his bruised rib cage. I was always careful to inform the class teacher and head teachers but my heart ached for them and I felt powerless and distraught.

Whenever I walked into a school building the smell was always the same. It took me back to my own school days and brought with it the feelings of being hated and of feeling stupid and incompetent. Thinking back I was a pretty useless supply teacher but at least I managed to keep everyone safe and the children seemed to like me on the whole. I had hoped that one day if I'd been able to teach full time with a class of my own I would be able to get over the old associations and learn how to be a reasonable teacher. I'd been told many times that only once you start to teach after qualifying do you really learn how to do it properly.

One Sunday, however, my therapist put an end to my aspirations by telling me I would never be well enough to teach full time. I was holding the door open for him after a therapy session and he stopped and examined my face. It must have been an expression of self-pity that prompted him to say, 'You are so severely mentally ill, you know. You'll never be able to teach. As for adopting children one day... I wouldn't even let you sponsor an elephant.'

My face must have fallen further and in response he shouted, 'YOU SHOULD BE BLOODY GRATEFUL YOU NEVER DID HAVE CHILDREN!' Aware that the man upstairs had opened the door to find out what was going on he lowered his tone and continued, 'From now on I want you to add another 200 voicemail messages every day to say "I'm grateful I didn't have any children who I would have damaged."'

I was quite relieved when I stopped the ad hoc supply teaching—no more having to experience the sinking feeling as I walked into school; a combination of feeling inadequate, never knowing what might happen and anxious as to whether I'd be able to maintain a safe environment. As for the end to my hopes of being a parent, I felt bereaved for the children I could never bring in to the world. It was a constant ache that never left me and I was very easily reduced to tears when the subject was brought up by an innocent comment from GPs or work colleagues.

Chapter 17: Dreamweaver

I took an extra shift at the investment bank I was working at in order to make up the shortfall from supply teaching. However, my therapist insisted I find more ways to earn extra income. I began to suspect then that the real reason for making me give up teaching was so that I could earn more money for him as the earnings potential from my design and copywriting work was substantially higher. He'd read an article on teleworking which was in its infancy in those days and suggested I look into working freelance from home to supplement my income.

I did some searches and found a website which followed the eBay auction model to match up freelancers with buyers who needed their expertise. Elance.com, or Upwork as it's now known, had just launched and so I set up a portfolio and started doing a few jobs online.

I rapidly established a small client base which grew by word of mouth, working tirelessly to provide the best possible service which included corporate identity packages, websites and content creation. I didn't charge them very much as I didn't feel my work merited a higher hourly rate as I'd never been formally trained in design or writing. I was hired for a web project and teamed up with a web developer named Luke.

Luke emailed me to ask if he could call me to discuss the project. When I spoke to him on the phone the first thing he said was, 'You sound lovely, what a beautiful voice'. We got on really well—too well—and started to chat for hours on end. I'd not heard of virtual relationships at that stage.

I was so excited to be working on the project with Luke. He liked my designs and I got him to do a bit of animation work for some of my clients. I convinced myself that it was safe, it was over the phone and internet after all and I wasn't doing any harm. But then I started imagining meeting up with him and projecting forward about how I might try to look a little less opted out than usual. I felt sick at the thought as I knew it would kill off even the virtual relationship as soon as he saw me. He wanted to meet me and I'd declined all along having made up a very implausible excuse about having had an operation on my knee.

Luke asked me to send him a photo and I asked for one in exchange. He was beautiful—almost too beautiful. I

didn't have a digital camera at the time and used up the remainder of a roll of film that I'd used to take pictures of my
cats; of which I had thousands. When I picked up the photos
from the chemist, I hurried home hoping I might have
caught a reasonable head and shoulders shot. I'd not seen
myself in a mirror since my therapist had banned it a few
years before. My hands shook as I opened the package and
took out the pictures of my cats. Then I gasped and broke
down in tears at what I was seeing. I couldn't recognise myself, my therapist had made me put on far more weight than
he'd told me. My face was swollen and puffy, my scraped
back hair made me look masculine, my eyebrows were wild
and a dark tinge above my lip clearly showed I needed to
wax it. There was only one photo of my head and shoulders
which didn't look as bad as the others so I sealed it in an
envelope, addressed it to Luke and dropped it into the post
box.

I expected that my photo would have deterred him
from even contacting me again but he sent me a sweet email
saying how much he liked my button nose. I started to feel
hopeful that one day I might be able to meet with him, even
be friends. Then at some point I froze and thought to myself,
'What the hell am I playing at?'

After the Mike affair and everything that had happened since, I would get no second chances. I would be told
to vacate the flat and to get lost—I knew it would be the end
of me. I just couldn't take the risk of continuing so I pulled

out of the project. I called Luke in floods of tears and told him I wasn't in a position to continue, I came clean about my background and about having therapy and told him I couldn't have any more contact. I winced to myself afterwards thinking he must have thought, 'What a f***ing lunatic'.

I posted a note under the door of the locked room to tell my therapist about Luke but he didn't mention it. I was scared he hadn't seen it so I mentioned about having had to stop the project because of falling in love with the web designer. Oddly he just took the mickey out of me. I suspected he hadn't read the full note though.

After a few weeks had gone by and in a moment of denial over my motives, I sent Luke an email, using the excuse that I needed his advice on some work. I apologised for contacting him out of the blue. He came back to me very quickly and said he'd missed me. The phone calls took off again and we'd be phoning each other several times a day again. I suspected he was happy to continue the pretence of a virtual relationship, but the guilt inside me built and built of course and I knew I'd have to end it again. In the end, I decided to ask him to meet with me before one of my night shifts in Bishopsgate in London. I knew that if he saw me it would be painful but would be the finish of everything.

We decided to meet at Liverpool Street Station. I recognised him straight away and I went up to him feeling anguished but putting on a brave smile. He was very sweet and didn't immediately look too shocked and kissed me on the cheek. I wore my charity shop black trousers, a burgundy sweatshirt and a black anorak, much less opted-out than I would usually wear but I could tell Luke was embarrassed to be seen with me. He told me to wait outside a bar while he went in to get some drinks rather than have me come in with him.

We chatted for a while then decided to walk up to where I'd be working. At one point I thought he was about to take us on a detour and I remarked on it. However, he completely misconstrued my innocent remark, believing that I'd thought he was leading me somewhere to be intimate. He had a look of absolute horror on his face. He muttered something about how we should have met up immediately i.e. rather than waste all that time getting to know each other only to be let down once we'd met. I said goodbye to him at the tube and felt the pain of rejection and humiliation deep inside my chest as I ran to the office in tears.

I struggled through the night at work and the next day I called him. He chatted for minute or so then said he was busy and had to go. It confirmed that my plan had worked. I didn't hear a peep from him again. The feeling of rejection was unbelievably raw and intense but I forced myself to go in to work that evening. I was in a desperate state. I sneaked off at one point and hid behind a huge photocopier away from the workstations and cried my heart out. After another painful day, my spirits lifted and I felt relieved and put the

thoughts of Luke out of my mind. The only emotion that remained when I thought of him from time to time was embar-
rassment and shame.

* * *

In the meantime, my therapist was continuing to pile
on the number of voicemail messages I had to leave. The
virtual relationship had taken up so much of my time that I
had been very careless checking that I'd left the correct
number of messages and would often miss some out accidentally. As result I was penalised with more and more. The
only way I could keep track was to set up an Excel spread
sheet with a grid containing the details of each message I
had to leave and boxes to tick to ensure I'd captured them
all.

Chapter 18: Neighbours and Uninvited Guests

For the 23 years I lived in Lewis Road I had relatively few encounters with neighbours (ignoring the brief liaisons with Mike). When I did interact, I did as my therapist told me, I didn't make eye contact and didn't smile or say hello. It was very unpleasant and my therapist would say all the time that if I did smile or chat I would be practising appearance addiction. From my neighbours' perspective I must have come across as rude and sociopathic.

The man who lived in the upstairs flat, Neville, despised me deeply and his girlfriends felt the same way. They would shout through the letterbox and scream with laughter when I walked past them in my opted-out clothes. When my huge, regulation knickers were drying on the line one day they shrieked at me from an open upstairs window and I felt so ashamed. 'Look at those f***ing disgusting pants, you f***ing ugly bitch.'

I used to receive hate mail through the post addressed to 'Miss A Tombstone' while I was working nights so they must have noticed my nocturnal tendencies. A car would come to pick me up each night just before midnight and I didn't return until 8am the next morning. My skin was deathly white from lack of sun and sleep.

While I was working on my laptop in the lounge one evening I heard an almighty crash and the sound of breaking glass. Someone had smashed the front door in. My heart leapt into my mouth and I stood frozen not knowing whether to run or call the police. In the end I ran out into the garden, locking the kitchen door. I was scared out of my wits and wanted to make sure my animals were safe but reasoned that the cats could probably run for it if anyone came in. I jumped over the garden wall into a neighbour's garden and then across another couple of gardens and out behind a block of flats. I ran as fast as I could to the nearest phone box and called the police. I refused to move until the police turned up and they assured me that whoever had kicked the door in was no longer there. That was all they were willing to do. When I told my therapist he was livid that I'd called the police. I was staying in the flat illegally and paying him rent so he didn't want any attention drawn to the flat. I didn't find out who had smashed the door in but wondered if it had anything to do with Neville. I wondered if he'd been trying to scare me into leaving.

I certainly wasn't ready to receive neighbour-of-the-year award either as I unintentionally enraged Neville from time to time. While I was trying to stay awake at night I would play spiritual music but often forgot to keep the volume down. I would also cook (and often burn) my food in the middle of the night which I know he couldn't stand as he'd light incense and burn it in the communal hallway. With my uncut hair that was so long I could sit on it, I managed to set it on fire numerous times by turning around too close to the gas hob. The smell of my burnt hair must have been absolutely revolting.

I drove him to rant madly upstairs and thump on the floor to try to make me desist from whatever I was doing to cause burnt food or hair smells. The floor thumping was used for all sorts of other reasons too. Feeding pigeons every day in the garden where huge flocks would settle on his roof and shit all over his window sill usually provoked the strongest reaction. Singing spiritual songs and a few secular favourites out loud in my kitchen came pretty close though.

While working nights, I endured a spate of break-ins to the flat while I was asleep during the day. I slept very deeply and so I'm glad I didn't wander downstairs to use the bathroom and bump into my intruders. It was such a horrible feeling to wake up knowing that strangers had been in the house and had rifled through my belongings. I had little of any value—my camera was taken once and my cheque book, credit and debit cards would be stolen each time. The ease with which I was broken into during the short time I was asleep during the day made me wonder if it had anything to do with Neville again.

Other unwelcome visitors included the bailiffs who came round on several occasions. This was because my therapist was nearly always late paying the rent on the flat that was owned by a housing association. Fortunately it was paid just in time before my furniture was taken away but it was very unpleasant to know that although *I* was paying the rent he wasn't. So I was at risk of having my things taken away and frightened of being removed bodily myself at any time.

Chapter 19: Sleep

At work, I was struggling to keep awake and it wasn't just because I was on a night shift, it was the sheer and utter monotony of leaving so many voicemails. I couldn't just dial and repeat the messages over and over on the same call; the rules were that I would have to hang up and redial each time and that meant 2,000 individual calls a day at worst. I was desperate to be able to stay awake so that I wouldn't lose my job and so I told my therapist how much I was struggling. Far from allowing me to have more sleep, he declared that I was a sleep addict and should have less sleep not more. He piled on an extra 200 messages to leave on his phones to say, 'Reminder to keep away from the first nod-off'.

My sleep was rationed from that point on and set at a fixed time. Undoubtedly there had been many times in the past where I just wanted to curl into a ball in my bed and sleep to escape my feelings: boredom, anxiety, isolation and procrastination were common triggers. But the underlying sleep deprivation made it so much harder to resist the urge. My therapist would phone me periodically to check up on me, yelling if he suspected I wasn't going to any lengths to stay awake.

Initially I was getting around 5 hours sleep a day. I worked nights for years, and always struggled to keep awake between the hours of 2am and 4am. During those hours my body decided it was going to get some sleep despite me. I would stand up to proof read work and my legs would buckle under me and I'd either fall forward and head butt the document stand or crumple to the floor. There were times when I would fall asleep in the middle of typing only to realise I'd filled dozens of pages with a single letter or digit. I wasn't the only one who fell asleep; Jerry, a tired father of four, once deleted an entire document by falling asleep with his finger on the delete button. Hugo, who was building up his own business during the day, would spend his breaks asleep under a table in a darkened room. He scared the life out of the cleaners at times.

Outside of work I lost count of the number of times I head-butted objects while falling asleep at home or while travelling regardless of whether I was standing up or sitting down. If I didn't fall forwards my head would snap backwards and I'd come to, gurgling and coughing. When I think of all the poor commuters I fell asleep on and occasionally dribbled on, only once did I have someone dig me in the ribs to stop me sleeping on her shoulder.

I remember frantically trying to fight the urge to sleep while I was at home trying to study for one of my Open University courses. My therapist made me keep the same hours as my graveyard shift at work and so on my days off I would have to sleep in the day and keep awake at night. It was bloody torture. I'd bought one of those kneeling chairs with no back rest which I thought would help me stay awake. I would sway back and forth on it drifting in and out of consciousness as I tried to fight the urge to sleep. While I was editing one of my essays, I fell forwards when my body decided it was going to sleep despite me and I woke up with a sickening crunch and horrific pain as my nose smashed against the top of my pc. Blood poured out of my nose and over the keyboard. I was more worried about how I would look with a broken nose than think about the absurdity of the situation.

During the 'wee small hours' as people used to refer to them, I would feel very depressed. I used to call it a chemical low as it didn't seem to be related to any particular event or feeling. I would think up ways of keeping myself awake such as washing the walls, picture rails and skirting boards, over and over, hoping that climbing ladders would deter me from nodding off. Instead I would plummet from the ladder, scattering cats as I fell asleep yet again.

My therapist would tell me to splash my face with ice cold water fifty times as soon as I felt sleepy. It certainly shocked me but the effects lasted only a few seconds and I'd be nodding off soon afterwards. I tried slapping myself around the face which was pretty hopeless as well. In desperation, I would leave the house around 4am and walk for miles along the high street and into Dalston and Shoreditch or in the opposite direction up towards Stamford Hill and into Seven Sisters as a means of trying to keep awake. I was cold and frightened of being outside the house at that time of night. I'd be able to kill a couple of hours that way and then come home, drink another jug of strong coffee and try to stay awake until breakfast and some blessed sleep.

I decided to see if there was anything that could help me to stay awake online and searched for natural remedies that might work. The essential oils I bought to sniff were useless but I did come across a gadget which was invented to keep long distance lorry drivers awake. I ordered two. They looked like Bluetooth earpieces and had some sort of motion detector built in so that when it detected your head starting to nod forwards it beeped very loudly in your ear. The gadgets did exactly that but in the end the beepers kept going off in time with my nodding head and I became oblivious to the noise.

I can remember the joy of seeing the sun rise during the years I worked at night and was delirious with happiness when I could finally lay my head on my pillow and sleep. When the alarm clocks went off for me to get ready for the night shift it would be dark already and I'd feel overwhelmed with sadness at having to get up.

On the journey home from work on the tube I would stand to keep myself awake and then fall asleep standing up. My knees would buckle and my head would hit the window over and over. Groups of people would be roaring with laughter at the sight of this odd woman keeling over and coming to with a loud bang as forehead met glass. It must have looked quite funny but the reality was very sad and I don't think it crossed my mind once to wonder why no one ever asked if I was okay. I guess they assumed I was drunk and therefore that it was self-inflicted.

In winter, with no central heating and wearing layers of clothes, two coats, a hat and gloves in the house I huddled around my paraffin heater. I fell asleep and slumped on top of it setting my clothes on fire. Fortunately I remembered a lesson at school and rolled around on the floor to put out the flames. A few years later when I could no longer buy paraffin from the high street—much to the dismay of my therapist who saw it as in keeping with living a humble life—I bought a halogen heater. You would think that the fear of setting myself alight again would prevent me from falling asleep, but not so. This time, I collapsed on top of the heater, burned my stomach and set my clothes on fire again.

I managed to change to a day shift and worked at the weekend in order to earn more money for my therapist and hoped that this might also enable me to stay awake. I was so happy to be able to see the daylight but the sheer number of messages I was having to leave by this stage, due to all my transgressions, meant that I was only managing to get two or three hours sleep a night. I would nod off several times during the day and would even fall asleep mid-sentence when I was talking to colleagues. My eyes would roll around in their sockets as I tried to keep them open and frantically attempt to recall what we'd been discussing. Despite this I somehow managed to do a very good job and worked at home to make up the time to ensure deadlines were met.

If I missed out any voicemails accidentally, or the voicemail system had failed somehow, I would be forced to use a day's holiday to stay at home and repeat the messages all over again. This happened on numerous occasions through the years. He would wake me up during my precious sleep time to rant and thunder at me for missing out some messages, 'WHAT THE HELL ARE YOU PLAYING AT? YOU'RE WASTING MY TIME!' I would be forced to get up, drink a jug of strong coffee and start my messages again from scratch.

I became very skilled at juggling phones in order to get the voicemails left on his mobiles as quickly as possible; something my therapist would have considered cheating. I had two blue-tooth earpieces hanging over each ear and two ordinary earpieces in each ear and dialled the numbers in rotation using the four phones. I staggered the dialling so that while I was leaving a message, the other phones were dialling in succession. At this rate I was able to leave the 2000+ individual voicemails which took me anything from

3 hours to 5 hours a day depending on how well I could fight off the urge to sleep. It was sheer, mind-numbing torture and began to feel like a total and utter waste of time and life. Often, once I'd finished the messages, I would fall asleep in my chair and then wake in a panic, realising it was time for work. My ankles would be swollen with fluid and my heart racing erratically as I spurred myself into action.

In my bedroom I had an exercise bike and an elliptical trainer and at one stage my therapist was annoyed that I was putting on weight despite the fact that my food portions were quite small relative to the other clients. He used to increase my exercise time so that he could increase my food portions. I was so exhausted that I even fell asleep pedalling full speed on the stationary bike. I tried so hard not to fall asleep but my body was weaker than my mind and the exercise bike and I would come crashing over sideways to the ground.

When I overslept one morning, my therapist was furious with me and insisted that I went out immediately to buy 20 old fashioned double-bell alarm clocks. I used to call them heart-attack alarm clocks as the loud ring would make me shoot straight up in the air with my heart in my mouth. Often I'd wake just before the first one went off but if I didn't, they would all go off together and I'd fly out of bed staggering around tripping over cats and empty guinea pig cages trying to silence them. The doorbell had the same effect on me and I must have developed an additional sense as I seemed to know when it was about to ring and I would wake up a few seconds beforehand.

On another occasion, I was standing up to stay awake while trying to leave the voicemails and accidentally dialled 999 on one of my phones while I was drowsy. I heard the operator say, 'Which service do you require?' and tried to hang up but couldn't. I apologised profusely saying it had been an accident. It wasn't long before I was nodding off again though and I managed to call them a *second* time. I quickly apologised and hung up but twenty minutes later, at around 3am, the doorbell rang and I could see blue flashing lights through the lounge curtains. Mortified, I answered the door. Two police officers stood in the doorway and asked if they could come in. I let them in and apologised profusely again and said it had been an accident and that I had misdialled and then managed to do it again as I was very sleepy.

The policewoman asked if she could check the flat and I was filled with the horrible realisation that they would want to see my bedroom at some point. They went down to the basement first and noticed the locked room by the bathroom but seemed happy with the explanation that my 'Landlord' kept it locked. Then they asked to go into my bedroom. It was the one room no one else saw and given how little sleep I could get, I hadn't cleaned it in months. I stood in the doorway looking at the floor ashamed while they negotiated empty animal pens, piles of clothes, bags of hay, clutter and exercise machines. Everything was covered in dust and animal fur. The floor around my bed had cups with spat out toothpaste in from where I'd cleaned my teeth in bed, too tired to go down to the bathroom. One of my cats was incontinent so I'd thrown the carpet away but the smell of urine lingered in the damp floorboards. I couldn't look the police officers in the eye but they seemed very kindly and unfazed and let themselves out.

When I tested my blood sugar first thing in the morning and after meals it was sky high. This was in keeping with the physiological changes that happen when someone is sleep deprived. All sorts of other weird phenomena occurred as a result too. One was an alteration in my colour perception. I would wake up and everything would be tinged blue for a while. I saw a neurologist to try to work out why the colours I saw kept changing and why I had a difference in colour perception from one eye to the other. After exhaustive tests and some MRI scans they couldn't find anything wrong with me.

Another strange phenomenon was lucid dreams. It felt like I was awake and conscious of my surroundings with my eyes wide open but I would see weird visions of people entering the room. I also had a recurrence of the sleep paralysis I'd experienced as a child. This was really frightening as I would be awake but totally unable to move any part of my body. I once tried to just relax and not fight it but I experienced a horrible floating sensation as if I was levitating. I remember wondering if this was what people mistook for an out of body experience.

When I Googled all the symptoms (and yes I became a chronic hypochondriac), all but the colour symptoms pointed to narcolepsy. Being unable to move yet conscious is often experienced by sufferers and indicates a disconnect in the brain between the conscious mind and the body's 'immobiliser' that keeps us from harming ourselves while we sleep.

Falling asleep and keeling over from standing up was another symptom. I looked into the type of treatment that was available and saw that a new drug had been put on the market to keep narcoleptics awake. Known as Modafinil, it seemed to be providing a significant amount of relief to sufferers and I wondered if this might be my only hope. The problem, however, is that it's a pretty powerful drug and when I saw the psychiatric side effects: mania, delusions, hallucinations and suicidal ideation, not to mention the physical side effects, I thought to myself, 'Well that rules me out then'.

However, I was so desperate that I wondered if a diagnosis of narcolepsy and short trial of a low dose might help.

When I pleaded with my therapist for him to let me have more sleep he said that as he was surviving on two hours sleep a night (because of all the work he had to do to look after me) why should I have the luxury of having any more sleep? He would say two to three hours was perfectly adequate. I decided to tell him there was a condition called narcolepsy and that I was experiencing all the symptoms of that. He said it was ridiculous and that, rather, all the people suffering from narcolepsy were sleep addicts. After brief mentions every few weeks for several months he finally consented and said I should see a specialist and so I asked my doctor to refer me privately as this was available through work.

When I saw the specialist I described all my symptoms but before ordering any tests he sent me away to fill in a sleep schedule. It was of course blindingly obvious why I was unconscious before my head hit the pillow at night, I was quite simply severely sleep deprived. The neurologist had told me that if sleep deprivation was ruled out I would then need to participate in a sleep study. Initially my therapist told me I should go ahead with the sleep study and lie about the actual number of hours I was getting for sleep:

'What the hell do they know about what's adequate' he would say, citing again his ability—as well as Margaret Thatcher's—to manage on two hours sleep. As this would mean a night away from home, however, my therapist told me to drop the idea and to never mention it again.

Chapter 20: Survival Tactics

Earlier, I mentioned that I felt I'd gone in to a protective, semi trance-like state when I first moved into my therapist's flat but looking back there were other areas of focus in my life which also helped me to survive his treatment over the years. There was the extreme obsession with my health, voluntary work with older people, my work and my cats.

I had always been preoccupied with my health, but since my confession it had become obsessive. Every lump, bump or neurological twitch would mean a visit to the doctor and often a referral. Over the years I had X-rays, ultrasounds, mammograms, MRIs, blood tests, ECGs and EEGs. I remember the excited dread I felt while waiting for the results. I don't think it was Munchausen's syndrome where a person pretends they have the symptoms and fakes it, rather I was making use of any anomaly to get it looked at and to hope it would be a real disease. Doctors would reassure me, believing that I was paranoid about being seriously ill. Little did they know that that was exactly what I wanted. It's a horrible thing to say this but I wanted something terminal like cancer.

I don't know how I put up with the MRIs. I have severe claustrophobia, perhaps related to being inserted head first into a sleeping bag and trapped in by my brother as a child. Either way, it would take several attempts to run the scan, much to the irritation of the radiographers. Clutching the panic alarm as I was fed into the tunnel, I would press the button in a frenzy to signal to the radiographer to get me out. With a fixed smile the technician would press her remote to bring me out of the tunnel, wait for me to psyche myself up, and insert me back again. The only thing that got me through in the end was a constant recitation of the serenity prayer[8] and keeping my eyes screwed tightly shut.

I ended up at accident and emergency several times. But, in all cases apart from the hyperventilation episode I described earlier, there *was* something wrong with me physically but mostly very minor things. On one occasion I felt so weak I couldn't stand up properly and was sent to hospital in a cab. I waited ages to be examined and when I was finally seen I knew the doctor thought it was all in my mind. I'm not sure if 'HYPOCHONDRIAC' was stamped all over my notes but the first thing he asked was whether I was feeling down. It infuriated me and I said that I felt really weak and dizzy. He rolled his eyes and then wheeled out a trolley of equipment, did some general neurological tests, ordered some blood tests, tapped my reflexes and even ended up examining my breasts. I was mortified at having my breasts examined, particularly as it seemed completely unrelated to my symptoms and when he sent for a chaperone I thought to myself, 'Oh for goodness sake I don't need an extra pair of eyes on them'.

There was more shame when he looked in horror at my unshaved legs and asked if I had a hormonal problem. I guess he'd never seen a dark-haired woman in her natural state. Finally he took my temperature and said with surprise and with a look that I perceived as scorn, 'Well you've got a temperature so I suppose there must be something wrong'.

A UTI was diagnosed and I was sent home with some antibiotics. I suffered chronic fatigue from that point on for the next couple of years which was very debilitating and meant lots of trips to the GP to be told it was psychosomatic. I genuinely don't think it was.

As with all obsessions it was a love/hate relationship. I detested the GP surgery and hospitals but my health obsession meant I couldn't stay away.

Each time it was the same: I'd find a symptom then obsess about it. I'd research the symptoms until I'd picked the one I thought it was. By that time I'd worked myself up into such a lather that I'd convinced myself it was serious and that I'd need a referral to a specialist. I had a diagnose-yourself book at first and later the internet to fuel my obsessions and knew all the signs and symptoms of a wide range of different ailments.

Then, for quite another reason I ended up being admitted to hospital in an emergency. Fleas were a problem in the flat with so many cats and I was also neglecting my hygiene somewhat so baths were infrequent and a daily wash at the basin sufficed in between. The fleas became horrendous at times to the extent that I could hear the tick, tick of them jumping on and off my books and papers as I lay on the floor trying to study for my degree. I could catch the fleas and pop them between my thumb- and finger-nails as a light grey, pus-like substance would burst out. It made me feel sick but there was a certain disgusting sense of gratification in doing it. My ankles were covered in flea bites and if you've experienced them, the itching is maddening. Having scratched one bite raw, I developed cellulitis around the bite. Clear lymph ran in torrents down my ankles and collected in my shoe. My ankle and foot swelled up massively and my lower extremity resembled a cross between a pig's trotter and an elephant's foot. Burning hot and purple, the only footwear I could fit on was a flip-flop.

I went to my GP who sent me to hospital and I was admitted and kept on IV antibiotics for a couple of days. My therapist was furious when he found out I was in hospital as it meant one of my meals was missed because of the emergency admission. He had a rather naïve understanding of treatment options and said I should have gone to see a private doctor for an injection that would cure it instantly.

As soon as I'd been admitted I thought immediately of my animals at home and the next morning, called a cat sitter to collect the house keys and feed the cats and change the litter trays. I then arranged to pay her to bring me some tins of food, fruit and my scales so my meals were sorted for the remainder of my stay.

On the second day, a consultant with a team of student doctors came to see me. The doctor seemed really excited and animated at the prospect of exhibiting my foot to her audience. When I drew back the covers, however, the disappointment was audible. My foot had already started to go down and didn't look anywhere near as bad as it had done when I was first admitted. I felt very embarrassed as if I'd let them all down and wasted the consultant's time.

While I was there I was put on a weighing chair, the type used for elderly or obese patients. I was so shocked to discover that my weight was two stone heavier than my therapist had told me it was. I was so shocked, in fact, that I convinced myself that the scales must be wrong. An accidental glance at a shop window a few months later told me that the scales were probably correct.

While I was glad to have been admitted and treated in hospital I was desperate to go home. I couldn't sleep at all while I was there and spent the nights wandering up and down the corridors pushing my IV bag along on its trolley; a back-wash of blood flowing from the plastic tube that led from the cannula in my arm.

A short while after my stay in hospital I decided to pay to see a private GP as I wanted to find out why I kept getting lower abdominal pain and was too embarrassed to see my own GPs given the number of times I'd been to ask for refer-rals. And of course I wanted to get it tested in case it turned out to be serious. However, I wasn't expecting the probing and questioning about other areas of my life. It had no place in my plans.

The first thing she said to me was, 'Do you mind hav-ing a beard?' I felt it like a blow to the chest, no one had ever said that to me before, I didn't realise it was that bad and I wanted to scream. The conversation then turned to my life and she probed around a bit and I gave her enough detail about my background, my food plan and therapist for her to say that I was being shut in a box and given no freedom. When she asked about relationships and if I wanted chil-dren, the outpouring of grief was instant. I sat there crying silently, tears flooding down my face and splashing into my lap. She mentioned a therapist that she knew of and sug-gested making an appointment for me. When she men-tioned his name I recalled an article that he'd written a few years before where he recommended patients learned to pamper themselves and have candle-lit baths. In my mind I rolled my eyes as I knew how utterly futile it would be to have a therapist who didn't have the knowledge about food addiction. Would a candle-lit bath do anything for a crack addict? No matter how kindly he might have been, I didn't take her up on the offer and didn't contact her again.

Over the years there were always enough symptoms to keep me researching on different diseases and illnesses pretty much non-stop. Looking back I now realise that I could see no future for myself. In my mind's eye I saw my life as a series of events along a winding road and the more despised I felt by my therapist the more the road had begun to fade into an inky blackness and I believed it was a foregone conclusion that I wouldn't reach my fifties. I think what I wanted was the drama of a big illness, the attention, sympathy and care from the hospital staff and an honourable way out of my life. Perhaps it was a variant form of Munchausen's coupled with a death wish. I could not go back to the hell of addiction and I was and still am far too much of a chicken to take pills or jump in front of a train. I did toy with the idea of an insulin overdose at one stage but wasn't sure if death would be painless. In addition, my therapist would say that suicide demonstrated the very height of self-centredness and selfishness. So instead I waited and hoped for a legitimate way to end my life.

* * *

Voluntary work was part of my therapist's recovery programme and was supposed to turn me from a self-centred person to someone who was able to be more caring and loving. This was a good thing. I made friends with some wonderful people in their 70s, 80s and 90s all of whom were very kindly and didn't flinch at my strange appearance.

Lily was the first person I visited and at 69 was relatively young to be in a befriending scheme with Age Concern (as the charity was then known). She had mental health issues and had spent most of her life in Broadmoor High Security Prison and then various psychiatric hospitals. She'd suffered with post-natal depression and had been convicted of trying to drown her baby daughter, Ruth.

I heard two variations of her story: one was that she was actually just trying to wash her baby in the river (she lived in a caravan nearby) and was mistakenly accused by a policeman who saw her. The other story, that Ruth had grown up believing, was that her mother had tried to drown her and the policeman had rescued and resuscitated her. Either way, there was neither acceptance of, nor provision for, post-natal depression in those days that might have offered her the chance to get help.

Eventually Lily was pardoned with the help of Ruth who successfully tracked her mother down when she'd reached adulthood. Ruth managed to secure a flat for Lily on the 20th floor of a tower block in Stratford, East London.

With anti-depressant medication Lily was able to live on her own with support from carers and health professionals.

Lily wasn't remotely bothered by either her appearance or how she came across. I think it was a good lesson for me. When I first met her, without announcing her intention, she hoisted up her loose crimplene dress and marched off to the toilet. She wore no underwear, perhaps because it was more comfortable and less effort to go without.

The smell of body odour in her small flat at the very top of the tower block was thick and overpowering and caused me to gag, especially in summer. Years of chain smoking, never washing and cooking smells had seeped into every pore of the flat, warmed and cooled, layer on layer, year after year. The carpets, the sofa with its rough, brown and orange stretch-nylon covers, the walls, ornaments— every item was covered with a sticky film that even her daily carers couldn't shift.

In her bathroom, the walls by the toilet-roll holder were covered in smears of various shades of brown where I assumed she must have wiped her hands on the occasions she'd run out of toilet paper. Her bath was pristine though and covered in unused scented soaps, bottles of bubble bath and cellophane-covered baskets of Body Shop goodies. Her carers must have bought them in the vain hope that she might have a bath.

I heard Lily pull the chain. She came out running her hands down the sides of her dress and walked into the kitchen to collect her fried egg sandwich and a cup of tea. As she drew on the cigarette that was hanging from her lip, Lily's face turned bright red, she forced her tongue out and exploded in a coughing fit. Eyes streaming and nose running, she pulled out a large grey handkerchief and wiped her whole face. Once she'd recovered she took another drag and walked back through to the lounge to sit on her favourite chair.

I remember clearly that first visit and was mesmerised at how she enthusiastically sucked and slurped her egg sandwiches and tea, I never did see her wear her teeth. The drugs she was taking for her depression and psychosis made her move constantly, body rocking back and forward, one leg twitching. They also made her hum continually in a flat, rhythmic monotone.

I remember asking (in as cheery a voice as I could muster) how she was doing but she didn't reply. I don't think Lily spoke to me for a good few months. She would sit in her armchair with a pile of blackened and thoroughly thumbed dictionaries piled on a table in front of her. She lived for her cryptic crossword puzzles and little by little as I turned up relentlessly week after week and month after month and sat with her in silence for an hour or so at a time, she started to share some of her crossword clues with me. Up to that point I'd never even tried to attempt a cryptic puzzle. She was good. I was pretty useless at first but started to get the hang of them and occasionally was able to help.

Lily's other two passions were Frank Sinatra and Princess Diana. The walls of her lounge were covered with newspaper clippings of both. On the day of Diana's funeral she and I wept silently as we watched it on the telly together. For Lily she was a beautiful, fairy-tale princess whose life was cut too short. For me, she shared the same illness and though she had never found freedom from her food addiction, she had found ways to relieve the self-centredness of her disease with acts of kindness and compassion.

Over the years I visited Lily, she opened up a little and would remark on news stories that covered child abuse or abandonment. I didn't open up to her about myself but it didn't seem to matter, I could share in the things she enjoyed and I grew to care for this little lady with her cropped grey hair and whiskers that put mine to shame.

After 10 years of visiting Lily every week, my therapist's utilitarian philosophy kicked in and I was forced to take some extreme actions in the name of caring. Lily had diabetes and didn't bother to take her medication or watch her diet and so my therapist decided I must insist on washing her feet and drying them carefully for her. My therapist had read that it was essential to keep feet clean and dry to prevent infections that might lead to gangrene and amputation. It felt weird to ask her and it felt like an intrusion to carry out but Lily agreed.

When I saw her toenails emerge from her slippers I had to muster every ounce of mental strength I could find to stop myself from vomiting. Mottled green and black in patches, her toenails were curled into spirals like snails' shells. The smell was unforgettable. After washing and drying her feet I arranged for a chiropodist to attend so that her toenails could be cut.

The next part of my therapist's strategy was nothing short of cruel. I was to use emotional blackmail to try to force her to take her diabetes more seriously. On my therapist's instructions I was to stop having any contact with her for a few weeks. I was then to go to her flat and tell her that I had watched my uncle die from the complications of diabetes and had been so upset about seeing her eating sweets and not taking her medication that I was unable to visit her. Then I was to say unless she stopped eating sweets and sugar I wouldn't visit her anymore.

During the weeks I stayed away, my phone rang and rang. Lily left message after message to ask if I was okay and to tell me she was worried about me. It broke my heart. When I was finally permitted to visit her, Lily was very upset and pretended not to recognise me. After a while she agreed to the ultimatum. A few months later, however, I found a huge stash of sweets hidden behind the toilet.

I wished I had never told my therapist about my findings as he decided that the next steps must be even more drastic. He said I should talk to her doctor and get her sectioned and put in a secure ward in a psychiatric hospital as he felt this was the only way to ensure her diabetes would be managed properly. I felt sick at the thought of what I was told to do but carried out his instructions. The doctor arrived with the necessary parties in order to section her. Lily was desperately upset which wasn't surprising after she'd spent most of her adult life locked away. The doctor told her that she needed to come with them to stay in hospital for a while.

Trembling and distraught, Lily took a stand and said she refused to leave her home. I was amazed at her courage and the GP realised that this wasn't a mental health issue but one of an interfering party—me. He was fuming with rage as he left with the social worker and psychiatrist.

Lily's eyesight degenerated rapidly because of her untreated diabetes and not long after the incident she was knocked down when she stepped in front of a lorry on her way to the optician. I went to see her in hospital in the early hours of the morning but she died a few hours later.

Esther, Ivy, Fred and Elsie became dear friends too and I visited them every week until they passed away. I was grateful that I had this opportunity to make friends with these wise and loving people. Towards the ends of their lives I would visit them in hospital and on a few occasions caused a fuss when it was obvious that they were being neglected. I would feed them as the nurses were in short supply and overstretched. At the very end I would sit with them and hold their hands. Though I doubt I was able to give them much comfort, I gained a lot from them and it was a good antidote to my self-pity.

* * *

As for my job, it became critical to my survival. My therapist was demanding more and more money which made me feel overwhelmed with anxiety as to how I could possibly earn more for him. As I mentioned before, I'd been working freelance as a copywriter and graphic designer in addition to the job I had at the time to try to supplement my income but I never felt able to charge people enough. The only thing I could think of doing was to change jobs and try to earn more. I spoke to an agency and was put forward for a position that would pay almost double my salary.

The hiring process was arduous. I had six rounds of interviews complete with a video conference to members of the New York team. The women on the team in London all looked, bar none, like models and I guessed that most of the people who interviewed me didn't want me because I looked so awful. My skin was pallid and spotty and though I didn't use a mirror I could see the reflection of the chin hairs in train windows and felt it like a body blow every time I saw them. I had a smarter than usual charity shop blouse and skirt for my interviews but when people first looked at me their faces reddened or they looked repulsed. I wasn't supposed to smile, make eye contact or let out my sense of humour but I did all three. I beamed for all I was worth and joked a bit to make them laugh. Even so the feedback from my agency was that they weren't sure I was a 'team fit'—a legitimate way firms can reject applicants who they consider odd. However, this was not the case with the man who was to be my boss. Mark looked beyond my appearance at my work record to date, the calibre of firms I'd worked for and my portfolio. Thanks to his lack of appearance prejudice, he backed me all the way, stood up to the critics and hired me. I don't believe I would have survived my purgatory without that job.

With what was going on at home you might think I would have walked around looking depressed and desperate at work but I didn't tell a soul about what I was going through. There was simply no point. A colleague who I worked closely with once heard my therapist screaming at me on the phone for some transgression. Other than that, however, no one had a clue what was going on outside work. Granted, I looked terrible, but I worked so hard and at such a high standard that I became a sort of national treasure among the slick and traditional city types.

I was asked to fly out to New York but my therapist told me it would be the beginning of the end of me and that it would be better to resign than agree. In the end I told my manager I was petrified of flying and asked if I could be excused. A few eyebrows were raised but I heard nothing more about it.

I kept myself to myself as much as I could and avoided social occasions that weren't compulsory. At the end of each quarter though, everyone had to join in with the celebrations. This was in the years leading up to the financial collapse in 2007/8. We would go bowling, play pool or participate in other activities and I used to love joining in and didn't feel guilty as it was compulsory. But I didn't tell my therapist. There were always photos taken of the events and as I had access to the drives they were stored on I would go through the photos and delete any shots where I appeared. Irrationally, I couldn't bear for them to remain and for others to see them as they looked through.

From time to time colleagues would bring in their new born babies for everyone to admire. I would be one of the first to ask for a cuddle with them each time. I remember noticing some fairly tough male colleagues looking at me holding the infants with quite a tender expression on their faces. I think they must have felt sad for me knowing it wouldn't be very likely that I'd be having my own.

I loved my work, it was everything to me. I set up the design and production department from scratch and built up a fantastic team of people over the years. So while I could escape during the day and totally immerse myself in my work, when I came home it would be back to the torture of leaving the voicemails and enduring the sleep deprivation and the relentless criticism.

* * *

I did still have my cats, however, and they were the only things worth coming home for—otherwise I would have gladly lived at work.

Every neighbourhood has a mad cat lady and that honour belonged to me. At one time I had six cats, a house rabbit, several hamsters and two guinea pigs. For whatever reason people become isolated, there's no doubt that animal companions can save lives. Mine were no exception. People used to say they were child substitutes. I don't think it was that simple. I didn't treat them like children, they were too independent for that, but I cared desperately and intensely for them with a physical ache in my heart when any of them went missing for even an hour longer than normal. When-ever I contemplated suicide, I would recoil in horror at the thought of my animals starving until the smell of my decom-posing body alerted the neighbours. It simply wasn't an op-tion.

I spent a fortune on vet bills, or would have done so had I not had pet insurance. Particularly so with Ron, who along with his sister Esme, was one of the two cats I'd brought with me from Tonbridge. With a sarcoma, which meant he had to lose one of his back legs, a muscle wasting disease and a brain tumour, the insurance company paid the bills time after time.

Although I adored Ron and I did baby him somewhat, with Esme, more than any cat, I felt an intensely deep connection. There was just something about the way she looked at me and perhaps how she felt in return. She was a fantastic goalie with pieces of crumpled up paper and would retrieve sprouts if I threw them for her. She was a dark reddish-brown tabby, with a deliciously soft, creamy tummy with light apricot-coloured spots. Compact and plump she would lick the back of my hand with her rough tongue and it would all but send me to sleep. She loved to stand on tip-toes on the palm of my hand while leaning over my shoulder so I could hug her.

When she was diagnosed with a lymphoma and given only a short time to live, the grief was instant and intense. I sat in the waiting room of the vets with tears streaming down my face and splashing on to her fur. The vet said she had a slim chance with chemotherapy but that it would probably be kinder to let her go there and then. I insisted we try and she went on a course of chemotherapy and steroids. Miraculously, she lived a further 15 years. When she was 19 she was diagnosed with kidney failure. The vet taught me how to give her sub-cutaneous fluids via a drip and by doing that twice a day, I managed to extend her life for another two years.

Billy, a small, all black cat, had turned up in my garden one day. His eye looked like it had been poked out. Actually the eyeball was there but destroyed although I never did find out how. When the eye healed, it looked like someone had replaced his eyeball with a large, overcooked hard-boiled egg. When I managed to catch him and take him to the vet, an operation was swiftly arranged to remove it and the socket was stitched up. He still had the blink reflex when I touched near his scar afterwards and once it was fully healed and the fur had grown over it, I used to kiss his empty eye socket, as if he might have some human emotions about feeling unlovable with only one eye.

I gave a home to my therapist's two cats, Cuddles and Ishka. They were such affectionate cats and were like a dear old couple who had been childhood sweethearts. They were devoted to each other, slept together, washed each other and offered each other morsels of food. I could see why Cuddles had been given his name too. He would climb up my body and put his forelegs around my neck and lay his head over my shoulder. He slept on me at night and often I'd wake up panicking for air with him fast asleep curled up on my face like a furry Russian hat.

Geoffrey, a street cat who had hung around my garden for a few years, finally joined the gang. He was a bully to my other cats and completely wild, slashing at my arms if I tried to touch him in the beginning. Slowly we got to the point where he would allow me to stroke his back and even put him in a basket to get him checked at the vets. I shouted and bellowed at him if he tried to attack the other cats and although I arranged with a cat charity to have him sent to a farm to live, I didn't have the heart to carry it out in the end. In time he mellowed and would sit on my lap. He never did lose his wild streak but he seemed to have a real sense of humour and even seemed to laugh at his own antics. For such a huge, rough, tough, street cat he certainly had a ridiculously cute, kitten-like meow which I think he had perfected. If you're a cat lover, you'll know what I mean when I say he was also a master of the silent meow.

My animals were my family and with vets trips, insulin injections, medication, toileting, cleaning litter trays and feeding, they plugged a large void and stopped me feeling lonely. I worried for them, cared for them and loved them all.

When my therapist found out about the cats sleeping on my bed he banned them from my room at night. Everything my therapist instructed me to do since my confession I had obeyed. But despite the guilt I felt, and the warnings my mind was issuing, I defied this ban and let the cats in anyway. If Cuddles was curled up with Ishka, Ron or Esme would take turns climbing under the duvet and would lie next to me instead, heads on my pillow, purring gently in my ear. If I felt down, there was always a sleeping cat to seek out, to bury my face in a soft tummy and inhale the warm, biscuity scent of their fur.

Chapter 21: His Name

For the first few years of being under my therapist's control I referred to him formally as Mr Karon and in my head (horribly patronisingly) as 'my little man'. Then having heard Shelley refer to him as 'Stan' I started to call him by his first name too.

After telling him about the liaisons with my neighbour and being told from that point I must leave a voicemail message telling him my every sick thought (the sin of omission being as dangerous as the sin of commission) he stopped me from calling him by his first name. When the number of voicemails became unmanageable, I remember saying, 'Please Stan, the messages have become so overwhelming, please can I have another punishment instead, please Stan I'm desperate'. To which he exploded 'STOP STANNING ME FOR CHRIST'S SAKE!' and added another 300 messages for my arrogance.

I was so scared of losing my abstinence that I even told him—admitting how ashamed I was—that in my mind I sometimes referred to him as 'my little man'. He looked like he wanted to kill me at that point.

So I ceased calling him by a name of any sort. Stan was short for Stanislaw, a name his mother had chosen after Saint Stanislaw I'm guessing. The more verbal abuse he threw at me and the more sleep deprivation or financial penalties he inflicted the more I wondered if he had either become corrupt or insane; perhaps I'd driven him insane. I couldn't bear to think of the name Stan anymore and the uninhibited part of my brain would insert an 'a' after the 'S'. To this day I can hardly bring myself to speak his name either silently to myself or aloud.

Chapter 22: Contact

From the point at which I severed connections with my family and for the next 16 years, my mother would come up to London periodically to try to visit me. She would sit for hours at a time in the car outside the flat hoping to see me. My therapist had insisted from the start that I was on no account to let anyone in to the flat. He said that if he came he would ring the bell three times—two short, one long.

On one occasion on a therapy day (usually a Sunday) my mum had been waiting outside for four hours, ringing the doorbell every 20 minutes or so. I sensed it was her but didn't answer the door. I was feeling sad and guilty but I was afraid of what I'd have to tell my therapist and the punishment I'd have to put up with if I were to let her in.

My therapist must have walked up the path and seen her standing on the doorstep ringing the bell. He told me later that he had pushed past her saying, 'You can't come in'. He rang the doorbell three times but realising he had his key on him, he opened the door and then shut it in her face and came into the front room. For the first and only time he looked a bit scared. He spoke in a low voice as if he expected that she might be waiting outside listening. He told me that she was only coming up to see me out of guilt and wanted to give the impression that she still cared.

I remember another occasion when I had just walked back from the station after work and saw my mother's car outside the flat. I quickly turned around and walked in the opposite direction and up to the high street to kill time for a while. I realised I would have to go home soon for my next meal so I walked back and then around the block hoping to sneak in from the other direction.

She spotted me and came rushing over. She looked haunted and sad, her eyes were red and staring. She spoke with a choked voice, 'Hello darling'. Secretly pleased but fearful of my punishment I let her come into the flat.

'I thought you might be ready to come back to us' she said several times. Such was the work that my therapist had done on my mind I just kept saying to her, 'I have no choice I can't, I have to accept what he tells me'. She gave me a hug.

'Sorry, I'm a bit oniony' I said feeling awkward that I'd been running around and was hot and sweaty. 'I don't care, you're my baby', she replied. I was frightened and agitated as my therapist was due to arrive any minute so I edged towards the door and she took the hint and left.

Fearful of being dishonest, I let my therapist know that I'd seen my mother. He was furious with me for letting her come in for a chat. He dictated a letter for me to send to her which said something along the lines of, 'Please don't come up again as it really upsets me when you do, if you do come again I won't be able to stop and talk but will go straight in'. I remember standing by the post box for ages not wanting to send it but I knew that if I kept anything to myself, the guilt would build and build and when I finally would have to tell him I knew the punishment would be severe. He had drummed into my mind that only complete and ruthless honesty would save me and that meant telling him my every thought, even the crazy, random, unbidden ones. My therapist used some powerful threats including weight gain, having the cats killed, crippling financial penalties and not least that I would die if I had anything to do with my family. This was enough to ensure compliance. I dropped the letter into the box, buried the pain and moved on.

At one point, if my parents had tried to rescue me I would have called the police, kicked, screamed and attacked anyone who tried to take me away from my therapist and therefore my recovery. I would have testified in court to support him. That was the crux of the matter, living as a practising addict is diabolical and despite what I'd been through and what was to come even the worst day in recovery was nothing compared to the best day in addiction.

My family sent me letters from time to time which, as I mentioned, I wasn't allowed to read. I would hand them over and hope that my therapist might be in an upbeat mood and want to share some of the contents so I could find out how everyone was. He would tell me that it was necessary to withhold the information from me and told me I had to be realistic about my parents' motivations. When he did refer occasionally to the contents of letters it was to ridicule and pour scorn on them. I remember he once criticised my mother for sending pictures of cats, telling me that she was trying to destroy me by targeting my weak spots. He said it would make a good Agatha Christie novel, 'She did it with cats.'

My therapist's verbal attacks against my parents grew stronger and stronger. Amongst my daily voicemail messages, I had to repeat 200 times, 'I'm grateful I'm not having anything to do with my parents which I couldn't survive'. Sadly, little by little, I started to feel indifference towards my family. Only at night time would I suddenly wake up, gasping with shock and with my heart thumping, wondering what the hell I was doing. I would feel desperately sad and would hear my mother calling my name in my mind. I would then hear my therapist's voice drown out my mother's, 'Candace, this is the easiest, softest option. You have no choice, if there were another way we would have found it. Remember, your parents have each other, you have no one. If it wasn't for them you wouldn't have this illness. They would welcome you back with open arms but you would lose your recovery and your life in no time. You simply couldn't survive without me.'

I could not go back to a life of addiction, so, accepting the cost of my recovery, I would roll over and go back to sleep.

Chapter 23: Quality of Life

My therapist's 'for the greater good' philosophy played over into all aspects of my life and one particularly traumatic area was with my cats at the end of their lives. With his abusive Catholic upbringing, my therapist believed euthanasia was a despicable act used by pet owners so they didn't have the inconvenience of having to care for sick and incontinent animals. To him we should not deprive any living being of one second of their lives without due cause. He detested the notion of quality of life being a deciding factor and believed that only God decided when our ends should come. Of course, he had threatened me with having my cats put to sleep to stop me chatting at work, but in that instance it would have been for the greater good because it would have stopped me from engaging in compulsive behaviour.

So instead of being able to arrange for euthanasia, I had to watch my beautiful animal companions suffer and die. Wouldn't it be wonderful if we all passed away peacefully in our sleep when our time came? Sadly, it doesn't happen like that in most cases. Billy, the one-eyed cat, died quickly of a heart attack but nonetheless cried out in pain. Geoffrey had a seizure and also died quickly but didn't appear to be conscious. With Esme, I took her to the vet after I discovered her collapsed and panting in extreme pain. I left her in the care of the vet with instructions to give her morphine for pain control while I was needed at a work conference for a few days. I hoped they would put her to sleep without my signed consent and when they called to tell me she had died I was at least relieved she didn't appear to have suffered.

For my other cats, although they were all given fentanyl patches (morphine-like analgesia) the vets wanted them to be put to sleep. On the threats of my therapist, I had to bring them home so that they would die 'naturally.' All died in agony or fearful panic as one by one their organs shut down. Bewildered and blind, Ron passed away on my chest as I lay in bed. I found Cuddles dead when I returned home from work, his face was contorted into a scream, a pool of blood by his mouth. For Collin, I was with him as he screamed and writhed in agony. I sat close to him, unable to comfort him while he went through his death throes. I wanted to tear out my heart in helplessness at his suffering, the sound of his cries drowned only by my own muffled screams.

After all the comfort and love I had received from these dear animals over the years, I was denied the chance to give them a small token of love by easing the most difficult of journeys that we all have to face.

Chapter 24: The Others

My therapist referred to the other clients as my sisters as if we were nuns who had taken a vow of silence. The expression used to make me shudder. Though I wasn't allowed to talk to or make eye contact with any of them, there were a few occasions over the years where I did have cause to have some interaction.

Belinda was working for a charity at the time and was asked to attend a disciplinary meeting. The accusations from her employers, a children's charity, included a lack of personal hygiene and rudeness to colleagues. They wanted to establish whether there was a physical reason for her poor hygiene and whether a diagnosis should be made to place her on the Asperger's/autistic spectrum to account for her apparent anti-social behaviour.

There was no doubt that when Belinda came over every Sunday to wait in the kitchen for her therapy session I always noticed an unpleasant but not extreme stale smell.

Belinda was far more obedient than I was to our therapist. At work, she strictly avoided eye contact and refused to talk to others unless it was directly to do with the work in hand.

Belinda was allowed to have a representative so my therapist asked me to attend to give her support. I took notes and was told not to speak. The managers described how her work colleagues had all complained about the smell in the office and she was told she must address the situation as well as attend a GP consultation to assess if there was a medical reason behind it. I was certain it was the charity shop coat she wore and our therapist's insistence that we used only unperfumed soap and water. Her employers also criticised her opted out clothes and told her to improve her appearance. Strangely enough my appearance was never mentioned in a disciplinary context even though the companies I worked at were all leading financial institutions.

Belinda spoke very patiently and politely to her accusers, told them she showered every day and explained how much she loved her job and the people she worked with. When she said that actually she preferred being at work to home I began to wonder if she, like me, also felt desperately trapped but believed she had no other choice.

I defied my therapist and spoke up about the apparent rudeness although I denied that I was aware of a hygiene issue. I said that Belinda had been a good friend for years and that it was just her philosophy to lead a quiet life and that far from being rude to others she simply wanted to do her job to the best of her ability and not get caught up in office politics. Not making eye contact and refusing to gossip was her way of leading a loving and spiritual life. This was a personal choice not as a result of a condition such as autism.

When I told my therapist that I had noticed the smell as well he shouted at me and accused me of being an enemy sympathiser, 'YOU'RE NO DIFFERENT FROM THEM, YOU JUST WANT TO ATTACK BELINDA'. Finally I found out later that he had conceded and allowed Belinda to use deodorant and scented washing powder to launder her clothes.

The next time I was to have anything to do with her was when I looked after her cats one Christmas. Copper and Amber were beautiful ginger cats and seemed to settle in well with me. On Christmas morning, however, I discovered that Amber had escaped and vanished. I walked the streets in the early hours, calling and calling but there was no sign of him. I was completely distraught. My cats were everything to me and to cause the loss of a friend's cat was devastating.

I did a leaflet drop and searched and searched over the next few days; but there was still no sign of him. Feeling hopeless, I then turned to the internet expecting nothing. However, the hope came alive again when I came across a forum on how to find missing cats. With the information I learned, an animal trap that I borrowed from an organisation called SNIP (Society for Neutering Islington's Pussycats); a night vision camera hooked up to a TV monitor and a book on missing cat behaviour I became completely absorbed in tracking him down. I spent night after night watching my monitor in my bedroom to see if he appeared in the trap. I sat there as various creatures with glowing eyes (as they appeared on the infra-red camera) entered and left the trap to eat the vast portions of cat food I'd placed there.

Finally, after three months of being on watch and viewing speeded up recordings of the times I wasn't able to be there, I suddenly spotted a cat that I hadn't seen before eating in the trap. He was about the right size for Amber. As it was via the night vision camera it was hard to tell his markings as all cats show their usually hidden tabby markings on infrared cameras. The trap was a manual trap which I could operate from my bedroom as I'd tied a very long piece of string to the catch. The string led all the way from the trap, through the garden and through my bedroom window, one floor up. I wound it around a bed post and kept some scissors close by. When I was sure he was busily tucking into the food inside the trap, I held my breath and tried to steady my shaking hands. I cut the string. Agonisingly, the string got caught and the noise it made frightened him off.

Anguished but undeterred I re-set the trap. The next evening as I sat poised with my scissors in my hand, he came back. With my heart racing I cut the string and this time the trap door closed. I ran outside to the garden, tripped over a spade and fell flat on my face. I scrambled up, barking my shins on a planter and ran over to the trap hardly daring to look and see if it was Amber. But there he was, as large as life, looking very frightened but very well fed. Belinda was overjoyed to have him home again and I floated around on a cloud of euphoria for days.

Rose was another 'sister' I had contact with after she was hospitalized with septicaemia. I took food in to her in hospital so that she could adhere to her food plan and also ran some errands for her. She went to extreme lengths to appear opted out. In addition to her dowdy clothes, old ladies' raincoat and knitted hats, she would hold her head to one side, protrude her jaw at an odd angle and mutter to herself. She made no eye contact at all to anyone. I remember my therapist saying she had led a jet-set lifestyle before and that these extreme measures were to counteract the years of superficiality and vanity.

She had been forced to leave her two young sons on the insistence of our therapist and it seemed to have destroyed her. She was made to live in a caravan on a farm and worked as a cleaner at the university nearby. My therapist told me how happy she was (and I've no doubts she was happy to be free from food addiction) but the constant bereavement she must have felt (and probably still feels) from having to leave her children must be unending torture for her.

Chapter 25: For What I Was Worth

Over the years the amount of money I paid my therapist increased steadily. My therapist said that he was taking on more people from North Wales and because of their very low salaries they weren't able to pay him very much. He said that those of us who were able to earn a good wage must start to subsidise our sisters. I remember seeing tears in his eyes as he told me how they would save a few pennies extra to give to him.

In addition, I had to pay on the spot fines for talking at work on top of the three quarters of my income that I paid him already and I also had to hand over any extra money that came my way. When my grandfather died and left me some money, I had to put all of it straight into his account. I once mentioned that I would like to try to save for a deposit to get a mortgage and after roaring with laughter, he dismissed the idea saying it wasn't in accordance with socialist ideals and that if I had any spare money I should give it to him so he could distribute it to his poorly paid clients. I had to get loans out for him, one after the other, of up to £10,000 a time, and although he initially would deduct the loan amount from his fees, within a couple of months his fees would go up more than the monthly repayment itself.

I remember once seeing a letter that came through to the flat addressed to my therapist which was franked with the name of an offshore investment company. Most people who hear about all the money he got from me would think it blindingly obvious that he must be pocketing it but it just didn't seem to fit. I bumped into him in various locations on occasion and each time he was always struggling along with a huge, battered suitcase containing umpteen bags of soya beans to give to those on low incomes and at least fifty mobile phones (twenty of which were used for all my messages). No, I think he had a kind of god complex. He seemed genuinely to believe that what he was doing was the ultimate good. He even implied that he was superior to Christ in what he had to put up with; the hard work he had to do; and the hours he had to spend each day dealing with addicts. He would joke about how Christ would at least be able to 'withdraw from the crowd' whereas he could never escape 'bloody addicts'. The other reason I felt he wasn't living a dual life was because of the reaction of the bank staff where I paid in money to his account. Their jaws would drop as they looked at his balance and one cashier offered debt counselling.

My therapist knew everything about my financial affairs and I had named him as my next of kin at work and as
the beneficiary of my life insurance. Knowing this, I wonder
now if he was trying to cause such physical and mental
trauma to me that it would kill me and his debts would be
cleared. He would definitely see my death as for the greater
good. I was causing him stress and that would have a knock-
on effect on his other clients. More money would mean he
could help more addicts.

What made me feel even more expendable was being
his 'body guard', walking up with him to the bus-stop close
to midnight every Sunday and walking back on my own. This
was Stoke Newington, with one of the highest rates of street
crime in the UK. Indeed, I'd been mugged several times in
my street since moving there.

One Sunday evening as I accompanied him to the bus-
stop, two men in hoodies approached us and one tried to
grab the mobile phone from my therapist's top pocket. I saw
a blade and shouted at my therapist to drop his phone. He
ignored me and continued to wrestle over the phone and
while he did so an envelope stuffed full of cash fell out of his
pocket. The men hadn't spotted the cash. When I saw the
blade flashing close to my therapist, I screamed for all I was
worth right in the face of the assailant. Very fortunately it
had the desired effect and both men ran off. I picked up the
cash and we ran the rest of the way to the bus stop. I waited
with my therapist until the bus arrived and then ran up to

the police station to let them know what had happened. They didn't seem interested. I had no money on me and was scared of walking home on my own but I had no choice. I decided to sing really loudly while running back hoping people would think I was disturbed and that it would deter the two men from approaching again if they were around still. Thinking back I'm not sure how I managed to survive the incident, I'm surprised I wasn't sliced open like a fish while I was screaming.

As time went on I sensed my therapist's hatred of me getting stronger and stronger. 'LOOK AT THAT FACE!' he would exclaim in disgust when I answered the door to him, no doubt it was contorted in anxiety and self-pity. The occasional crumbs he used to throw at me, such as to wish me a happy birthday, had long since stopped. He trusted me less and less and would check up on me constantly. He insisted on seeing my payslips and when he saw that the 75% of my income that I paid him didn't include my national insurance contributions or non-contributory pension scheme, he launched into a vicious attack telling me how deceitful and dishonest I was.

I couldn't speak. Adrenalin pumped round my body as I boiled inside. I had told him everything, given him everything he asked for, taken out loan after loan for him, told him my inner thoughts and believed without a shadow of a doubt that I had held nothing back from him. I had been entirely and ruthlessly honest.

'You sod, you absolute f***ing bastard!' I raged to myself but my face must have betrayed me. He looked as if he wanted to hit me and approached with his arm raised but checked himself. He never did lay a finger on me, he didn't need to; his voice was enough and he used it like a weapon.

Chapter 26: Breaking Free

My father said to me years later that if I wrote down my story I should call it 'The Golden Goose'. He believes strongly that money was the sole motivator for my therapist and that ultimately he pushed me too far. For me, it wasn't the money, the screaming at me at all hours of the day and night, not the control, not the constant criticism nor even the separation from my loved ones that finally led me to search for a way out, though all these factors contributed. In the end it was the sheer torture of leaving more than 2,000 voicemails every day coupled with the desperate sleep deprivation. I really felt that I would have to find a way to live on my own as I knew I couldn't physically survive his regime for much longer. To continue to adhere fully to my food plan was a no-brainer, but to somehow find a way to live in the real world was the desperate hope.

I think my therapist was always deeply disappointed in not being able to break my will and constantly told me that I was nothing like the others, had a monumental ego and was bitterly disappointing and a waste of his time. He used to say to me often

'IF YOU DON'T DO AS YOU'RE TOLD YOU CAN GET LOST.' But he knew I was dependent on him; that I believed I couldn't survive without him.

My therapist looked ill and exhausted and said I was exacerbating his diabetes. He would scream at me every night because I just couldn't keep awake to leave the voicemails. He often caught me out as he would track me as I left the messages so that he could clear them at the same time. If there was too long a gap between the messages I was leaving, the phone would ring and I would wake with a start, bracing myself for the verbal assault as I picked up the phone. I would drink a whole jug of strong coffee and stand up to a high table and even march on the spot to try to keep awake but inevitably my legs would buckle under me and I'd fall over and invariably hit my head on something.

I was shattered. My blood sugar levels were sky high, I was nauseous and hallucinating. There was no time to do anything— the flat was a mess as I could only just keep on top of the washing up and laundry. When my dear cat Esme, died at the vets, I collected her body meaning to bury her straight away. Knowing it would take me ages to dig deep enough to prevent the foxes getting to her (and I didn't want to see her dismembered body scattered over the lawn as I'd seen with Collin), I had no choice but to wrap her in bin liners and make room for her in my freezer. She was there for three months before I finally got the chance to dig her grave.

When my therapist told me I'd caused him to have a mild heart attack and was responsible for the deaths of two of his clients because I took up so much of his time, something in me snapped and I started to break the rules and stopped confessing my transgressions. I started to read books that were forbidden. I devoured the Harry Potter stories and then started to watch children's films while leaving the voicemails, plugging my laptop headphones into one ear and juggling four mobile phones while I did so with the Bluetooth earpieces perched on each ear as well. I justified children's films because I reasoned that as I was a qualified teacher it would be useful if I ever went back to teaching. Kids' films grew rather boring in the end though and the fact that I wasn't telling my therapist meant that I was giving myself more and more permission. Soon I was watching any films I could get my hands on. I joined the local libraries and on my way home from work picked up two films to watch every night.

Now I could escape my monotonous life, the isolation, disappointment and the bereavement I felt for the loss of my younger years and the children I always wanted. Gradually I stopped wearing my headscarf on my head and wore it around my neck instead. I started to wear clothes from the cheapest high street outlets rather than charity shops. I bought a nicer pair of glasses and shoes that were a little more fashionable. One colleague at work said I looked less like a peasant farmer from the old Soviet Union.

The films kept me awake so I could leave the voicemails at the same time and get them all finished in record time. I watched hundreds of films, from Harry Potter to box sets of 24 and the West Wing. It was so exciting. I think my therapist felt I'd turned the corner and had submitted my will at last. I no longer met him at the door with a self-pitying expression and I no longer had the calls in the night. I did feel guilty though but pushed the feeling away. Only at night did the guilt feel so overwhelming that I had to sleep with the lights on for fear of what my conscience or perhaps God might be trying to tell me.

Carelessly, I had hidden a DVD cover of the box set of Lord of the Rings along with a Smallville video behind the books in my bookcase and he found them and confronted me in the usual manner. He even described Smallville as pornographic. I hardly flinched now when he screamed at me and I think he sensed it. So he started to force me to make all 21 meals for the following week in advance on a Sunday and then would insist on checking every meal, digging around in my food containers with a spoon, counting every single one of the twenty plus vitamin tablets I had to take. I think this was his way of forcing me to use up any spare time I had left at the weekend.

In the meantime my letters to my mother became a little more friendly and started to include the words 'Dear Mum' and 'Love Candace' and I even sent them a Christmas email with some news about the cats. They responded and I kept them up to date a bit more. I did this without mentioning a word of it to my therapist.

Despite the films, I was coming to my wits end with the messages and the sleep deprivation. I made the decision one day to do something I thought would be a huge risk. I had been forbidden to read any literature about eating disorders and bulimia or food addiction as I was told it would endanger my life because I would be led astray. I also had heard that overeaters anonymous was no longer using a food plan which is why I felt there was nothing out there that could help me. I genuinely believed my therapist was the only person in the world who could help but I thought I would just try to Google 'food addiction' and see what might come up.

Instantly I saw three websites which talked about food addiction. The first was Kay Sheppard's site, then FAA (Food Addicts Anonymous) and then RFA (Recovery from Food Addiction). They all had a weighed and measured food plan which avoided binge trigger foods and were very similar to the one I was on. I decided to send each of them a message describing the situation I was in with my therapist. The message was long but I needed to get across the fact that I wanted to find another way to live in recovery but was scared and desperate to protect my abstinence. I received a reply from all three. The representatives from both RFA and FAA sent me messages telling me to contact my GP. I was dismayed. Then I received a response from Kay Sheppard herself. Here is the email I sent and the response I received from her.

In a message dated 2/6/2010 1:08:07 P.M. Eastern Standard Time, candace@candaceh.orangehome.co.uk writes:

Hi Kay,

I've been abstinent from food addiction for 23 years with a private therapist. Initially things were great but now I feel he's become so extreme that I feel I'm only existing. Couldn't bear to go back to the hell of bulimia but very sad as things stand. I've put a timeline of events from start of recovery at 21 (sorry bit long) and am told that surrendering to his will (practising humility) is my only hope and the main weapon against addiction and that I'll die if I try any other approach.

Below then is my story, grateful for advice. I live in the UK and afraid of trying something else or picking a group that might harm.

Candace

Timeline:

17 anorexia giving way to bulimia up until I was 21, couldn't hold down a job, smoked 30 a day and was a wreck. Saw family doctor who sent me to various therapists but none could address the bulimia.

21 went to private psychotherapy became abstinent from food addiction via adherence to food plans

22 was married

23 told by my therapist I was in a bad relationship and must leave him so I left husband and moved up to London to flat owned by one of therapist's clients. Still live here not allowed to leave.

24 to 28 continued to see therapist, got good job still abstaining from Bulimia. Another client moved in to share flat with me.

28 had relationship with man who was married, felt guilty told therapist was severely reprimanded and told I couldn't see my family any more was able to send notes to them but not allowed to read any letters sent from them. Was told I had to put on weight and to take the Pink Paper to work so people would think I was gay. Told if I had contact with my family I wouldn't survive and would binge.

28 to 30 qualified as early years teacher but told by therapist not ready to teach so gave up teaching

30 grandfather died left money which therapist said he needed to help others (so those on low income could also follow food plan regime)

33 told that I would have to give my cats away if I didn't stop talking socially at work (told that social interaction is deadly for bulimics who are food/appearance addicts)

30 to 44 therapist started to make me leave voicemail messages reminding me to do things including a gratitude list daily which included things to remind me of my bulimia and also to say i was grateful to God not to see my parents because it would kill me.

Told that lady who used to be flatmate had killed herself and it would happen to me if I left.

The messages have become 2,000 a day which takes me hours to leave, get very little sleep, nodding off at work and home. But if caught nodding off therapist shouts and screams at me and gives me more messages to leave. The focus of my therapy now revolves solely around the quality and accuracy of the voicemail messages I leave and am continually told I would have died if not for the messages. I have 20 mobile phones which costs me £500 a month. I'm told that because I cause him so much stress I gave him a heart attack and led to the deaths of three of his clients who left him as he wasn't able to give them enough attention.

I now have to pay 75% of my income. This I'm told is because the others my therapist sees can't get high paying jobs and some are jobless so this is a 'socialist' system of wealth distribution.

I'm not allowed to socialise, have relationship, have children, read newspapers, TV, television films. Am supposed to pray and meditate and work. Not allowed to own a car or bicycle. Told I must surrender to his will and do as I'm told as this is the only way a food addict can survive.

Because I couldn't keep awake to leave messages I started to watch TV programmes with ear plug in one ear whilst leaving messages at the same time. Since not doing exactly as told is now making me start to doubt if he's gone from helping to extremism.... wonder if this is the only option.

I would rather die than go back to the hell of active bulimia, and for many years was happy with my life but now feel am just existing. Having looked on net seems that more understanding is being made that like an alcoholic, food addicts can't eat certain foods without it setting up a craving for more. There seem to be various treatments out there that accept the wisdom of adhering to a food plan but without such extreme lengths.

Would like to know if I should continue (given how severe a mental illness food disorders are) as I am (better the devil you know) or take the risk of finding another group or specialist.

Kay's reply:

----- Original Message -----

From: KShepp825@aol.com

To: candace@candace.orangehome.co.uk

Sent: Saturday, February 06, 2010 6:34 PM

Subject: Re: Therapy becoming extreme

Candace, you are not in a good therapeutic relation-ship--I think you know that. Go to my website and join my loop in order to start interacting with sane people. I think you need to find support to detach from your controlling therapist. I will be glad to help you any way that I can. And I want to tell you that in therapy I give people tools so that they can manage their own lives, not depend on me for every decision. You have been controlled by this person so long, I think you will need a strong support system to detach from him.

Warm regards, Kay

P.S. Please describe to me how you manage food.

After a couple more exchanges where Kay had asked me if my parents would help and after I confirmed that I thought they would she suggested that I should get away as soon as possible. I was afraid to act but she said she would help me. Kay is a certified mental health counsellor and eating disorder specialist and although I hadn't read her books at that stage, the fact that she had 35 years of recovery herself at that point and had helped thousands of others gave me so much hope that I began to feel butterflies in my stomach. Perhaps there was a way after all to follow a food plan and put away the sack cloth and ashes.

Having received the response from Kay, I then sent my parents the following email:

Dear M and D,

I've been starting to question my therapist's methods as they've become very extreme. I started to search and see if there was an alternative system of staying away from the awful bingeing and throwing up cycle. It seems that finally it's recognized as a chemical imbalance in the brain and that the treatment is to avoid trigger foods, adhere to a food plan (the good part of my treatment) and attend support groups just like people who go to AA but not to do the extreme things that I'm currently doing.

If you read below you'll see a response to me from a lady who founded a food addiction recovery programme http://www.kaysheppard.com/ and below that a timeline of my recovery from 21 to date. I hope this might start to help you see why I haven't had contact, why I left Neil etc.

I'm trying to work out how to transition to a different regime and wanted to ask if I needed to (i.e. can't find myself a flat to move to quickly) if you could bear it if I (Maisie and Mr M) could rent a spare room with you till I can sort myself out. I totally understand if you don't want me to after what must have seemed years of extreme callousness from me.

I'm not sure if I'm brave enough nor where to begin though as I'm afraid that I've become so 'institutionalized' now that any sudden wrench without a support network might be the finish of me. Blood pressure gone right up just thinking about it. It's been hammered in to me that there is no other way so I'm scared out of my wits plus I'm likely to feel very guilty given that he did save my life. Plus maybe I've needed to be hounded by someone.... I'm sure you can remember how slothful I was and how I stooped so low as to steal food from Jane and her children.

Hope you both are ok and Mutt you enjoy seeing Ferg and his family in Israel.

Love from Candace

After I sent the message I got a reply from my mother saying I could use my brother's old room. Then I received another from my father saying he thought it would be a good idea to come up with the truck immediately given that my therapist was due to come over that evening. I decided to act and phoned them.

I still had all my voicemail messages to leave for the day and hoped and prayed my therapist wouldn't find me out and call me as I didn't feel strong enough for a confrontation. I then wondered if he suspected anyway and would come over early in a cab. So I packed up my clothes, put my two cats into their baskets, grabbed a few possessions and tried to clear up a bit before my parents arrived.

By this stage I was living in squalor. With only two to three hours of sleep a night and the rest of the time working or leaving voicemails, the flat was in a horrible state. For the first time in years I was able to really appreciate the grim dwelling I'd been living in. After two of my cats were incontinent at the end of their lives I had no carpets left in the flat and couldn't afford to replace them. The floor boards were stained with cat urine and stank. I had kept guinea pigs in my bedroom and still had straw and droppings under the bed even though they'd died of old age a few years beforehand. The guinea pigs also produced a weird kind of dust that covered everything: furniture, bookshelves and books. There was a bird's skeleton under the bed which one of the cats had brought in. The poor bird had gone through the complete decomposition cycle with the help of bluebottles. Where the man upstairs had flooded his bathroom, a huge chunk of ceiling had fallen through and everything was damp. My mattress was mouldy from the flood, covered in cat hair and filthy from cat-flea faeces.

The damp basement was equally grim. There were no carpets here either and there were tiles falling off the bathroom walls. The brand new toilet looked out of place and didn't fit the hole the previous loo had occupied. I had to have a new one installed in an emergency as I'd fallen asleep on the old one that wasn't secured down properly and as I fell asleep sideways the bowl came with me and smashed all over the floor.

On top of the makeshift cupboards in the basement were black bin bags tied and stacked to the ceiling and must have been full of my therapist's belongings. They had hissed and buzzed for weeks as whatever was in them was consumed by maggots and flies. Some maggots had escaped, scaled the wall and cocooned themselves at the point where the wall met the ceiling. They had never emerged as flies though and their dusty coffins had been there for years. It smelled terrible but I was forbidden to go near the bags.

In an odd cupboard above the landing, which could only be reached by a ladder, was an old fashioned gilded bird cage and a packet of shot-gun cartridges.

The doorbell rang. I was desperate that it would be my parents and not my therapist. I saw a glimpse of white hair and saw my father first, then my mother and then a tall man I recognised as my brother-in-law. Relief soon gave way to shame knowing that they would have to come into the flat and see the mess but there was work to be done. I kissed them all and I think I must have looked distraught. We packed my father's pick-up truck with a few belongings, a large sack of soya beans, my laptop, a chest of drawers and a few books. My father also picked up a crate of paperwork which included bank statements and itemized mobile phone bills the size of pre-internet telephone directories.

I did a quick check of the flat and realised I would have to leave most of my things behind. I tied the door keys on to a ribbon and hung them so they could be reached through the letterbox so that my therapist and the two other women, who came for therapy sessions on Sundays, could get in.

I then wrote a note and left a final voicemail for my therapist telling him I had found another food addiction recovery programme and that I did not want to feel responsible for causing him another heart attack or that my behaviour might lead to the deaths of any more of his clients. I climbed in to the back of the truck with my two surviving cats and we drove away.

Chapter 27: Coming Home

When we pulled up to my parents' house my sister was there waiting. She congratulated me on having had the courage to leave. I didn't feel very courageous, just fraught with anxiety as to whether my therapist's predictions would come true.

I don't remember very much about the conversations we had that night but I think I started to try to let my parents know why I had let my therapist have absolute control over me. My father mentioned Stockholm Syndrome as an explanation and my mother said she understood why I had to stay away but said that she had felt sure that one day I would come back.

I wanted to tell them there and then but couldn't find the words to explain that I couldn't change the past, or get back the years or take away the immense strain and grief I had put on their relationship. However, I was determined to do everything I could to be as loving and supportive as possible from that point on. I wanted to tell my father that he was a hero for what he did and for being so swift and decisive.

I emailed Kay to tell her I was with my parents and she arranged for us to have a call the following evening. That night I lay in a soft, comfortable and clean bed. It smelled of fresh fabric softener and the sheets and duvet were ironed. The ceiling above was whole and white. My cats lay under the bed—Mr Malinky snoring reassuringly. Had I done the right thing though? My heart thumped and thumped as I tried to sleep. My therapist had predicted my parents would welcome me with open arms but that I would be dead within a matter of weeks.

Early the next morning I sent an email to work to let them know I had to leave my flat suddenly and was staying with my parents but would be in the next day. I had switched off all my mobile phones and called the various networks to let them know that I wanted the phones cancelled with immediate effect. It took nearly two years to finally pay the last of my mobile phone bills as I was locked into 24-month contracts. I spoke to IT at work and gave them my therapist's numbers so they could block any incoming calls but I gave no explanation. It would have to be a completely clean break.

I went downstairs and had my usual breakfast. I was okay and my heart was calm. I felt an overwhelming sense of relief at not having to leave any voicemails. I took a cup of tea up to my parents and watched them sleeping in their giant bed. They'd aged but they were still my dear old 'Mutt and Dod' as I used to call them before I was banned from using any terms of endearment to refer to them. Stretched out on his back lying next to my mother was Matthew the cat, sleek and black, paws gently kneading the air.

I had my phone consultation with Kay and let her know immediately that I was concerned as I kept hearing my therapist's words replaying over and over in my head. I had been made to write and repeat on voicemail hundreds of thousands of times over the years, 'I'm grateful I'm not having anything to do with my parents which I couldn't survive'. Kay's caring but no nonsense approach kicked in and she taught me there and then some cognitive tools to help deal with negative thoughts and self-fulfilling prophecies. I was to ask myself to think about the thoughts underlying any particular episode of negativity. Then I was to ask myself if those thoughts were either true or useful. If neither applied, I was to simply reframe the issue in positive terms and repeat it to myself many times. Here was the process and affirmation:

> Kay: 'What's the feeling?'
> Me: 'Fear'
> Kay: 'What's the thought behind it?'
> Me: 'My therapist said I would lose my recovery without him'
> Kay: 'Is it either true or helpful?'

Me: 'No'
Kay: 'So what would be a more positive thought to
replace that one with?'
Me: 'Erm, I take responsibility for myself…?'
Kay: 'And how about adding, "and as a result I am
happy joyous and free from being out of control, one
day at a time"'

I was told to write, read and record it forty times over.

Over the next few days, every time feelings of fear began to bubble up, I called to mind the affirmation. Within one or two repetitions, the feelings of anxiety faded and I felt calm and reassured.

The simplicity of the approach astounded me and I began to apply what is known as Rational Emotive Therapy on every occasion I felt down or negative in any way. Who'd have thought the spoken word (aloud or inside our minds) could have such power? The power to make us spiral downwards into despair or to climb out of negative thinking into a feeling of calm and happiness.

I was amazed at how quickly I adapted to my new life at my parents' home and after just one day off work, returned to the office and had to tell a few white lies about my circumstances. Over the next few days, a strange feeling was building in my chest, one I wasn't familiar with. It was joy.

It grew quickly over the next few weeks and was joined by feelings of hope and anticipation.

My brother-in-law said later that when he had come up with my parents to bring me home, I had looked like a stunned wild animal, haunted, hunted and wide-eyed with shock. The next time he saw me a few weeks later he couldn't recognise me. I was smiling, relaxed and happy.

Chapter 28: The Suicide Gene

I ordered Kay's books, '*Food Addiction: The Body Knows*'[9] and '*From the First Bite*'[10] as well as her book on daily affirmations '*Food Addiction: Healing Day by Day*'[11]. I'd always looked down on the notion of affirmations but I was seeing the hard evidence for myself that they worked amazingly well.

I read *From the First Bite* first of all and came to the chapter on causes. Now my heart was racing for a good reason as I read that there is hard scientific evidence to suggest that addiction is a biogenetic disease. I could no more change the colour of my eyes[12] than change the gene responsible for my addiction. It wasn't my parents' fault that I was a food addict (apart from passing on the genes they carried). And while my therapist's food plan had enabled me to be free from practising addiction, his bullying, abuse and psychological torture had done nothing to help me mature emotionally as an adult; to be able to deal effectively with feelings and be able to live in the real world. Though I learned to care unconditionally for others it came at a huge expense to the happiness of my family and my mother in particular.

I absorbed the knowledge and evidence that Kay presented in her books in just a few weeks. Here was finally the truth. I didn't have to walk around in sack cloth any more, reciting Thomas à Kempis constantly in my mind and on voicemail. I no longer had to avoid eye contact and suppress my smile and didn't have to live in forced isolation.

Kay adapted my food plan to one with more healthy portions and a greater variety of foods. I had been eating the same meals over and over for breakfast, lunch and dinner of soya beans, hard boiled eggs or boiled liver with fruit and vegetables. But now I could have more of a variety which included brown rice, sweet potatoes, all manner of pulses and grains, fish and chicken, vegetables and a slightly decreased variety of fruit as some fruits are too high in naturally occurring sugar.

In addition to the food plan I started to work a more comprehensive 12 step-based programme of recovery. Until such time as a person's genetic make-up can be manipulated and cured of addiction, there still needs to be certain measures and practices a sufferer undertakes on a daily basis to prevent a return to disordered eating and denial of the nature of addiction. Food addiction is a disease that affects the body and the mind, so without a programme to challenge negative self-talk we automatically start to slip back into old habits and patterns of thinking.

Getting enough sleep (not excessive sleep) is also an essential part of the programme and I was getting a full seven or eight blissful and restful hours sleep a night and was exercising more healthily. I started running a couple of times a week during the lunch hour at work. I felt alive and full of energy for the first time in so many years. I stopped falling asleep at other times during the day and while I wasn't even thinking about my weight, it adjusted to a healthy and stable level.

I continue to be amazed at how quickly I adapted to life outside of my therapist's prison. I also had felt, like Kay, that I would need a strong support network to detach. But there it was in front of my eyes—my family, Kay, her books, phone meetings and some self-help tools.

Chapter 29: A Life Expanding

A month after my escape, I flew over to Denmark for a weekend retreat that Kay was running. This was the first time I'd been out of the country let alone on a plane in 20 years. I'd booked an apartment to stay in for the trip with a full kitchen to prepare my meals in comfort. I arrived the day before the retreat was to begin and had a short walk around the town centre. It was so exciting and I couldn't believe my change in circumstances.

The next morning I got a cab to the retreat which was held at an addiction rehabilitation centre in Copenhagen. I walked in and recognised Kay from the photo on the back of her books. She was getting her presentation ready on her laptop and I greeted her and told her who I was and gave her a big hug. She looked very happy and a bit taken by surprise but I didn't care, I was so grateful.

Kay is a gentle, down-to-earth, beautiful lady with a ready smile and a wealth of compassion. She has a determination to speak the truth and give out the critical information that food addicts need. What made her knowledge and philosophy all the more compelling was that she herself is a food addict and has been in recovery and binge-free for nearly forty years to date. She told me she had had her DNA tested and sure enough the variant gene that's believed to be responsible for addiction was identified.

I learned even more on the retreat and watched some videos on research into the dangers of refined foods. One called 'Sweet Suicide'[13] showed how deadly and addictive all forms of sugar are. Rats fed on sugar showed the same withdrawal symptoms as those fed on cocaine, for example. Though there's a wealth of information about how deadly refined sugar is, there's also a very powerful food industry that's more than happy for customers to become addicted to their products.

At the end of the retreat I exchanged contact details with some of the Danish women who were at varying stages in their recovery. Kay went home to Florida and I went back home to Chislehurst, delayed by the ash cloud, but so happy to have made the journey.

I got to know my family all over again and met nephews and nieces who I didn't even know existed. My sister who I was estranged from and who I had resented over the years because she didn't have the disease, I came to know as such a lovely person, an amazing mother to her beautiful children and a dear friend. Together with her husband and three children they are now so precious to me as indeed are my two brothers and their families.

I saw my 'baby' brother again after all that time of separation and hugged him tight. I had loved him dearly when I was his younger big sister and felt the loss of not seeing him very keenly. Being able to travel with my family to the south of France to celebrate his wedding was wonderful.

I hugged my cousins, uncles and aunts again. Sadly some relatives had passed away during the years and I had no knowledge of their passing because of having my post confiscated.

Much later I contacted Shelley's sister and arranged to meet up with her at a coffee shop in London. I had hoped that given the lies my therapist had told me over the years that he might have been lying about Shelley's death too. Sadly, Shelly's sister confirmed that she had indeed taken her life and we worked out that it wasn't long after my therapist had told her to get lost. Shelley had planned her suicide so that she could not be found or resuscitated. She rented a room in a flat in North London and there took her life. She left a note to say that she was, '...sick and tired of being sick and tired'. Not long before, Shelley had sent me a letter but I was doing exactly as I was told at the time and pushed the letter under the door of the locked room in the basement. I'll never know what it said. I remember watching my therapist as he would pull an 'oh dear naughty me' face when he spoke of her from time to time. It sickened me.

Five months after leaving the flat in London I met Simon. Kind, funny, unique and with bags of common sense, he didn't seem fazed in the slightest by my food plan or my bizarre background. I decided to tell him very quickly about my regime so that he was fully aware of my priorities and could beat a hasty retreat if he wanted to. I let him know that my recovery has to come first and that there can be no negotiation on my food plan and programme just like someone with renal failure must put their dialysis first to stay alive.

His background couldn't have been more different to mine and he was unlike any man I'd ever dated. We became friends and it wasn't long before that wonderful time when we said, 'I love you' to each other. Critically, he supports my food plan and has never complained about what I do for my recovery or the time I spend helping other food addicts.

In September 2010, I secured a mortgage to buy my first home. I was now, of course, able to keep all of my salary and save some every month and with a loan from my father and brother I was able to put together a deposit on a tiny terraced house in Tonbridge. A home of my own—I could hardly believe it. By Christmas, Simon moved out of his flat and joined me.

We now live near the coast in a home we love with a beautiful countryside view from our bedroom which goes all the way down to the sea. Sleep at the moment is disrupted at times but for good reason. At the beginning of 2012, Poppy and Daisy were safely delivered by caesarean section and in my arms after a full-term uncomplicated pregnancy at 46. Twins! Poppy with blond hair, blue eyes and slightly pointed ears like a pixie and Daisy with golden brown hair, dark brown eyes and dimples like her daddy. Finally one of the things I'd dreamed of but long since given up hope on had become a reality.

I remember saying to my mother how sorry I was for the pain she went through for so many years. Only now that I'm a mother can I appreciate how desperately your heart aches just imagining what others must being going through when separated or bereaved through the loss of a child. That's how she felt, bereaved but with no closure. 'But look what you've given us now' she said as she cradled my two girls gently in her arms one day.

I still work for the same firm and all but my closest colleagues think I just had an extreme make-over. 'What's your secret?' they would ask me as if I'd teamed up with a personal stylist and fitness coach.

The weight loss that resulted from the small adjustments to portion size and a more healthy food plan meant that I had to buy new clothes a few sizes down. I was fearful when I initially confronted my reflection after such a long time avoiding it but things were different now. I had the understanding of the genetic nature of my disease and realised that my obsession with my body and appearance was a symptom, not the disease itself. I now had the tools to work on any negative thoughts about what I looked like and how I came across. I bought clothes I liked and that seemed to suit me. Not a trace was left of the old feelings I had as a teenager of yearning to be tall, fine-boned and willowy. I just wanted to be the best version of me that I could be. I started to apply a small amount of make-up and got my eyebrows shaped and had my hair styled.

Eyes widened in surprise when colleagues I hadn't seen in a while saw me. I got lots of compliments but would change the subject gently as I didn't want my appearance to become the all-consuming focus it once had been for me. It was simply a nice side effect of a healthy food plan. I would think to myself, 'I've just escaped from 23 years of slavery and am at last able to celebrate recovery from food addiction *and* live life to the full and yet people think it was just about trying to look better.' But how could anyone think otherwise when I'd kept everything to myself?

I've no doubts that that my job and my colleagues played a huge part in saving my life over the years. Since leaving my therapist on 7th February 2010, my happiness and therefore my confidence in my position at work grew markedly and I was promoted to marketing director and more recently MD of marketing. I went on the first of several trips to the New York office and on sales and marketing meetings to Germany, Holland, Italy and Portugal.

My life today is dramatically different. I feel like Rip Van Winkle might have felt after waking from his sleep. Not just family but actors, news readers and politicians seemed to have aged overnight. In a generation, I missed so much about world affairs and I'm still catching up on news and events that happened during that time.

I also feel like a radically changed person and looking back it's as if I've led four separate lives, the angst-ridden child, the soulless, mindless addict, the hostage and now the still very much flawed but self-aware and happy person that perhaps I was meant to be.

During the first three years after getting away from my captor I tried on several occasions to write about my experiences. Each time I started to write a few paragraphs I felt the fear build inside me again and decided it was best not to continue. On the first couple of attempts I had recurring nightmares about seeing my therapist for therapy and pretending I still lived in the flat, wondering when he'd notice I wasn't leaving him messages any more or paying him any money. Worse than that was a recurring lucid dream where I believed I'd woken up in the flat and my daughters had been taken away from me. I couldn't get out and all the windows and doors had been boarded up from the outside. I would wake up in a blind panic until a wave of relief would wash over me as I realised that all was well—my husband lying perched on the side of the bed, me on the other with our two girls spread eagled between us.

The last dream I had was quite recent, I was walking through some woods with my daughters and I had the feeling I was being followed. Absolute fear set in and I pushed my girls to the ground and shielded them with my body. Someone was trying to drag the girls away. I tried to scream but couldn't make a sound, I tried again and again and in absolute anguish I managed a small moaning noise which slowly crescendoed into an almighty scream. It was so loud, it broke through my dream and into reality and frightened the life out of my poor husband. After that it felt like I had somehow turned a corner from fear into resilience.

In my spare time, on my commute and in the evenings, I do what I can to spread the message of recovery to other food addicts through sponsoring and helping at meetings. And whether they are of the non-purging type or bulimic the treatment for all food addicts is the same: a healthy food plan that cuts out trigger foods combined with a 12-step based programme of recovery.

My Body

Where once I detested my body—my thighs, my breasts, my bottom and stomach—pretty much regardless of its size, today it's my dear and faithful friend. Robin Korth sums it up beautifully for me:

'...As I looked in the mirror—clear-eyed and brave— I claimed every inch of my body with love, honour and deep care. This body is me. She has held my soul and carried my heart for all of my days. Each wrinkle and imperfection is a badge of my living and of my giving of life'. [14]

My Ex Therapist

A few people have said that they believed that my relationship with my therapist demonstrated a clear case of Stockholm Syndrome where a strong emotional bonding can form between an abuser and their victim. Perhaps it played a part at the beginning after the trauma of separation from my family but post my 'fall from grace' I think I put up with the abuse because I believed there were no other options or similar treatments. Whether saint or psychopath, my therapist had thrown me the only lifeline that was available to me at the time. And, though it meant causing pain to my family, my philosophy seemed to be that the greater harm would be caused by my own death from my disease, versus the harm I would be causing by having no contact.

I found out recently that my parents were so desperate at one stage while I was away that they hired a detective to try to find out more about my therapist. However, Mr Karon used several names and that must have made him hard to track down. My father said that they had had to give up and were advised by their church minister that if I wasn't ready it would be hopeless and dangerous. I would agree with that entirely as I used to be paranoid about the possibility of being kidnapped, bundled blindfold into a van and driven off to a psychiatric ward with well-meaning but ignorant treatment centre specialists trying to make me eat normally; pumping me full of addictive trigger foods and tranquilisers.

At the moment I have accepted the fact that I will continue to live with dual feelings towards my therapist, knowing that without him, there would now be a fading plaque in a rose garden in Beckenham Crematorium. Had I known about Kay Sheppard's programme back in 1987 things could have been very different.

At times I've wondered if perhaps I needed the bullying for all those years to keep me away from addictive eating. But I've seen for myself the dramatic changes in people who have become abstinent with other programmes. I've seen how working the 12 steps, working with other addicts and using all the tools that enable thought patterns to be changed is what keeps us in recovery rather than guru-like individuals who foster total dependence. It is the willingness to admit defeat over our drug of choice which forms the basis of a gut-level acceptance of our powerlessness over the first bite, sip or fix. In addition is the much needed but gentle ego deflation that comes about through relating to a power greater than ourselves.

I've often thought about the others still being dominated by Mr Karon and whether to contact them to let them know there's a life out there waiting to be embraced. To let them know that a healthy programme exists that can enhance and strengthen their recovery. But I fear that direct contact would do them more harm than good. If Mr Karon is still operating, I hope that Belinda, Rose and the others may get the chance to read this book so that they may be aware that there are other choices open to them. While our recovery is paramount, it needn't come at such a high price.

PART III

Chapter 30: Recovery in the Real World

The remainder of this book includes a discussion of food addiction, genetics and brain chemistry as well as an outline of the recovery tools and references that have helped me. If you or others you know are affected, I hope this will help you to find the correct information without having to resort to unhelpful or abusive practitioners.

What is food addiction? Kay Sheppard describes it as '...the compulsive pursuit of a mood change by engaging repeatedly in episodes of binge eating despite adverse consequences.' [15]

If you're a normal eater, those who binge must seem stupid, irrational, deranged or just plain greedy. Why can't they just eat healthily? 'Everything in moderation!' or the more extreme I've often heard, 'What's wrong with these f***ing people?'

For the same reason an alcoholic taking one sip of alcohol is compelled to drink to excess, so the food addict, on ingesting addictive trigger foods, is compelled to eat until they can't fit another morsel in. Dogs, intellectually disabled people and binge eaters have one thing in common: they are able to eat until their stomachs rupture.

Thousands of people have been helped with 12-step programmes for food addicts. However, personally I have seen the strongest recovery with Kay Sheppard's food plan and programme. The plan is constantly monitored in conjunction with medical professionals and adjusted and revised where necessary. Kay herself is a Licensed Mental Health Counsellor and Certified Eating Disorder Specialist. She believes in stabilisation not traumatisation in therapy sessions.

Kay's books and website contain almost all of the necessary information for people to start to recover. In addition a large community of recovering food addicts participate in a Facebook[16] group, exchanging ideas and support. Support can take the form of answers to questions about the food plan in the early stages of recovery and is a place where food addicts can request a sponsor and sponsors can offer their services on a voluntary basis. Undoubtedly, though, there are some food addicts who would need to stay at a treatment centre to get over the initial cravings and this can be achieved at centres which are open to using food plans that avoid trigger foods.

Users, Abusers and Addicts

For those who simply can't understand why someone would eat and eat until they're stuffed to bursting point, it can help to split people into three groups: users, abusers and addicts.

Users, enjoy their food but have an 'off button', a functioning appetite which tells them when they've had enough. They truly comprehend satiety. Users can eat for comfort at times but revert to the norm again. A food addict may watch a normal eater discard half a biscuit and find it totally incomprehensible.

Abusers also enjoy their food, they just eat too much and usually become obese, particularly as they get older. Abusers may eat for comfort too. Health issues usually compel them to curb their eating eventually. However, they can control their eating if they have to. A taxi driver once started sharing his health issues with me and told me that he had to have quadruple bypass surgery. I asked if heart conditions were genetic in his family and he said 'No, I was eating crap and needed a kick up the backside. I eat mostly fresh fruit and vegetables now and I've lost 10 stone'. I would call him a reformed abuser.

I would suggest that many abusers think they are addicts but if they're able to pull their lives together, stop using or even moderate without a programme then I doubt it. Abusers who've cleaned up their lives can be dismissive of those who are truly addicted, 'I got over using drugs, why can't they?'

Sheppard states: '...not all overeaters are food addicts. Using the diagnostic criteria for drug use to differentiate those who have control over addictive trigger food (drug) use and those who do not, the former group can be diagnosed as having "substance abuse" and the latter can be diagnosed as having "substance dependence". Substance dependence and addiction are interchangeable terms. The consequences of both abuse and dependence are often similar and always serious, but the conditions are different in cause and treatment. [17]

A Biogenetic Brain Disease

For addicts, their bodies are genetically predisposed to react to certain substances[18] (sugar, cocaine, and alcohol for example) in the same way over and over. Food addicts don't want to over eat—their body hijacks their minds and compels them to. One small amount of trigger food is enough to cause an exaggerated spike in dopamine in their brains; far higher than for normal eaters[19]. However, these high levels can't be sustained without further ingestion of the substance. In its absence, dopamine levels then crash, compelling the addict to seek out more of the same. And so the cycle repeats over and over until the addict is stuffed to bursting point or their eating is disrupted. Most food addicts eat in secret, ashamed of their gluttony.

So what causes the brain chemistry to become out of kilter? Dr Ernest Noble, at the University of California[20] has discovered mutated versions of the D2 dopamine receptor gene in the DNA of addicts. These alleles are believed to be responsible for carbohydrate craving and compulsive eating. In a study of 70 obese patients, over half of them carried the rare A1A1 or A1A2 alleles. The more common or 'normal' version of the gene is the A2A2[21].

Without this critical knowledge, a sufferer can only blame themselves for being weak-willed. Well-meaning health professionals often cite low self-esteem as one of the causes of eating disorders. It's hardly surprising that sufferers have low self-esteem given the extreme behaviour of bingeing, throwing up and spending hours on the toilet suffering the effects of laxative abuse. For many who aren't terribly successful at throwing up and aren't physically able to run off all the food they've ingested or for those who have had the disease for some time and find that self-induced vomiting can no longer compensate for the increasing amounts consumed, the weight gain is also a source of shame. Those who binge but don't purge are often labelled as having Binge Eating Disorder or BED. Without being able or willing to vomit their food, the frequency of bingeing is limited by the stomach's capacity. For all food addicts the norm is fasting or bingeing, punctuated only by sleep or work if they are still able.

Until recently, there was little solid scientific evidence to explain why some people lose control over the amount of food they eat. Without scientific evidence, the general public, as well as most scientists and physicians, have argued that food addiction is something other than a disease. The result has been that policy makers fail to understand the nature of food addiction and often blame persons with the addiction for the addictive behaviour and its consequences. Food addiction has often been addressed and often unsuccessfully treated as an 'eating disorder' or trivialized and treated as a weight-loss issue. [22]

Not all food addicts are obese and likewise not all obese people are food addicts. A normal or overweight food addict who purges or exercises to excess is identical to the extremely obese food addict who has to be lifted out of a building by a crane. The only difference is the extreme measures they go to in order to avoid putting on weight, driven by their equally extreme obsession with their appearance.

Born or Made?

This is one question that I didn't dare to ask myself for many years after my ex therapist had said it was not only false but dangerous to even think about the possibility of food addiction being a genetically determined disease. To him parents or guardians were responsible for creating addicts. From the recovery meetings I've attended, the one thing I've noticed, time after time, is that the backgrounds of the members couldn't be more diverse. Sure, some of the people have come from a violent background with alcohol or drug-dependent parents; living in poverty and being subject to bullying, abuse and neglect. However, an equal number have also come from affluent backgrounds with parents who showered their children with love, good schools and nourishing meals. My therapist would say that the hidden abuse of middle-class dysfunctional families was often more harmful because it involved silent neglect, shaming and a lack of unconditional love.

Far more compelling for me is the scientific evidence that points to genetics as the cause and of being the common denominator that brings together the many disparate people who attend 12 step meetings. Regardless of their starting point—some reaching their rock bottom while drinking non-beverage alcohol with a baby in their arms for example—they have been transformed from wretched, dangerous and despairing addicts to eloquent, funny and compassionate people.

Further evidence shows the similarities between the brains of drug addicts and those with 'eating disorders'.

"...In the past two decades, scientific evidence has emerged that affirms that food addiction is a chronic brain disease that can be treated successfully. We have come to understand that Food Addiction is a Biogenetic Brain Disease. Functional MRI scans have revealed similarities in the brain chemistry of drug addicts and chronic overeaters—

studies which have gained the attention of the National Institute on Drug Abuse.

Recognizing that a condition is a disease—brain chemistry that is out of balance—and not self-imposed or resulting from lack of will power, helps to reduce social stigma and leads to more research and improved treatment outcomes.."[23]

A baby born with the faulty version of the dopamine receptor gene is born an addict even though the symptoms of the disease only become apparent over time. I very quickly learned to use food as a means of blotting out my feelings because it gave me such an instant feeling of euphoria. However, my own acceptance and realisation that there was something very wrong with me was only apparent when I could no longer satisfy my cravings with the limited quantities of food that were available at home. In other words my disease had progressed to the point at which I was no longer getting the same high from the same quantities of food; I needed ever more and more. Once I had begun to steal food and money to obtain my fix I was confronted with the undeniable truth that I was very sick.

It is interesting to note that people with the faulty dopamine receptor allele have far fewer receptor sites than normal folk, hence the reason for using substances to feel better. It so happens that there's also an inverse correlation between body size and dopamine receptor sites[24]. Dr

Kenneth Blum coined the phrase Reward Deficiency Syndrome in 1996 to more accurately describe addiction as the breakdown of the reward loop in the brain. It is the deficiency of the reward response that drives an addict to relieve their chronic state of brain chemistry imbalance with all the consequential aberrant behaviours they undertake in their quest. Perhaps when DNA testing becomes routine, early detection and intervention could help to prevent a generation of Wednesday's children becoming tomorrow's fully-fledged addicts through elimination of refined and processed foods in their diets. For more information on the biochemistry of food addiction, follow this link http://kaysheppard.com/articles/the-biochemistry-of-food-addiction/

The Age Myth

Stereotypically, sufferers of food addiction are considered to be young girls and teenagers. Probably because that's the age the disease often starts to manifest itself and GPs' advice is sought. But what happens to them once they hit their twenties and beyond? One huge myth is that these girls 'grow out' of it. Not so. There are bulimics in their seventies and eighties who are still suffering or have finally found a solution having been on thousands of diets, visited countless therapists and tried all manner of treatments. They have spent a lifetime in and out of treatment centres. Many have substituted drugs or drink for food but, ultimately, if they manage to recover from these, their number one addiction, food, comes back to haunt them. At their worst, I have heard of older bulimics bingeing and inducing vomiting up to 20 times a day. There is no let-up; they become gorging and purging machines. Finances, relationships and sanity are destroyed.

Other food addicts don't make it out of their teens. I mentioned Nicky, one of my school friends who drowned in the bath after starving, bingeing and purging. I've known others who hanged themselves to escape their torment and another well publicised case of a girl, only 15 years old, who lay down on railway tracks and ended her life because she just couldn't face her disease any more.

Anorexia giving way to bulimia

Many food addicts have experienced a period of controlled starving which led them to become very thin. They were probably labelled anorexic but then they flipped into binge eating and purging with episodes of starving in between. It is estimated that 50% of people who have had anorexia develop bulimia or bulimic patterns[25]. There are those who continue to starve themselves and either die young or die earlier than most through heart or other organ failure, malnutrition or suicide. It's worth repeating that eating disorders are the highest cause of mortality among all mental illnesses[26] and also to mention that 20%[27] of people diagnosed with an eating disorder will die prematurely from

complications related to their disease. It's such a hideous illness that often suicide seems the only way out. The mortality rates for food addicts as a whole are very hard to gauge,
however, as it's often the medical complications of death
that are reported rather than the eating disorder that com-
promised someone's health in the first place.

People with anorexia, who restrict their food intake
but don't binge, may or may not possess the normal dopamine receptor gene. And though they may not be food addicted, the very same weighed and measured food plan has
been successfully used to treat anorexics as this takes away
the fear of loss of control. If they are serious about recovering, they can adhere to a plan, knowing it will look after their
bodies and prevent their weight from becoming too high or
too low.

Intuitive eating

Many specialists believe that people labelled with an eating
disorder should be encouraged to eat normally through a
process of learning how to eat intuitively. And of course why
wouldn't we all want to eat normally if we could? However,
it's my firm belief that true food addicts (and it's very likely
they would all be shown to have the variant dopamine receptor gene), are, quite simply, physically incapable of eating normally because of the way refined and processed food
acts on their brains. A weighed and measured plan, free
from trigger foods (which tend to be the same for all food

s away the fear of loss of control. It also takes
)f putting on too much weight and enables the
_ ;o of the decision to choose portion sizes and
therefore either under or over eat. The kitchen scales will
maintain a healthy body and bathroom scales can be thrown
away as they cause unnecessary anxiety and feed the obsession with weight.

Why doesn't gastric bypass surgery work for food addicts?

It seems like a no-brainer to suggest that surgery to reduce
the size of the stomach would be the answer to addictive eating. You simply can't fit all that food into your stomach.
Many food addicts, full of hope and expectation, go through
this mutilating surgery, experience the elation as they lose
weight initially only to find themselves back to the same
weight or higher than before. But now they have other
health issues to contend with, not least of which is constant
diarrhoea and the risk of complications post-surgery. The
underlying issue, food addiction, hasn't gone away because
it has very little to do with hunger and appetite. Although I
would be hungry after starving myself for a day or so, hunger
was rarely the trigger for my binges. I would be ravenous but
it was the effect of the substance I ate that led to the excessive amounts I then went on to consume. And, while it's true
that those who've had surgery can't binge in the same way
they used to, they find other ways, such as non-stop eating

of sweets and chocolate so that highly concentrated, high calorie consumption takes over from periodic volume eating. This is in much the same way that the old procedure of jaw wiring led to patients melting down confectionery and drinking it through a straw.

Why does the food plan work?

A weighed and measured food plan is the equivalent of abstinence from alcohol and drugs. You can't just stop eating in the same way that you can stop using drugs and alcohol. It isn't enough either to just stop eating binge foods. This is because food addicts have problems with managing volume as well. Weighing and measuring and sticking to a food plan means that sufferers don't have to judge portion sizes any more. This is essential because their 'off button' is broken and appetite means nothing to them. Food addicts eat whether they're hungry or full. In addition, there must be a good balance between complex carbohydrates and protein. Protein is essential for keeping brain chemistry in balance.

Critically, the plan also ensures a sensible calorific intake which enables the metabolism to function at its optimal rate. This is in contrast to those who restrict their intake severely and therefore cause the metabolism to be shocked into starvation-prevention mode.

Following a food plan can, quite simply, give sufferers freedom from insanity and a progressive and fatal illness. It isn't easy but it is possible—travelling and social occasions can be managed with good planning. Those desperate enough to get better now have a programme for living in the real world. It can be managed with children, a full time job and voluntary work on the side.

Putting the cork in the bottle

Total abstinence from known trigger foods is currently the only successful way for a true food addict to recover. Once addicts have gone through the detox from addictive foods— and for many a honeymoon period of feeling on top of the world—they are suddenly left with raw emotions that they've never had to deal with before due to constant anaesthesia with food. From childhood or youth, most food addicts have looked to food to blot out all feelings—from extreme highs to crashing lows. I ate for comfort at such a young age that I have no recollection of feeling any strong emotions from that point onward. Sheppard describes this as bypassing the emotional maturation process[28]. Bodily addicts are adults, emotionally and spiritually they are toddlers. It becomes easier to eat food that gives them a high than feel the pain and learn how to cope with it.

After detox and into stabilisation, the work then needs to begin to rewire the addicted brain so that sufferers can learn to deal with negative emotions and learn how to change them to positive ones. The food plan isn't enough on its own—a recovery programme is required as well. This is because the addictive substances that were used over and over provided a shortcut to the brain's reward system. According to Berke, JD, et al. overuse of addictive substances '...caused the hippocampus to lay down memories of this rapid sense of satisfaction, and the amygdala created a conditioned response to certain stimuli. Stressors or something associated with substance use can [therefore] trip the mental machinery of relapse.' [29]

A magic bullet?

With the knowledge as it currently stands of the roles of brain chemistry and pharmacology for, say, depressive illnesses it might seem obvious to assume that medication will provide the solution for addicts of all types. Drugs that act on dopamine receptor sites, then, might seem to be the way forward. But, so far, there has been little long-term success. Existing drugs interfere with the brain's motivation and reward system but the memories persist so that the addict still wants the high. Drugs which have blocked dopamine receptor sites and therefore render drugs such as heroin and cocaine ineffective result in an addict craving a high but getting no satisfaction, 'Neutralizing the pleasurable effect of the drug is not enough because reminders of the drug experience perpetuate the longing and cause addicts to stop taking the counteracting medication'.[30] As a result many scientists believe that for drug addicts (note that food addiction has not yet been widely acknowledged) recovery programmes and behavioural therapy will still be critical. Scientists cannot doubt the efficacy of the 12-step programmes even though one of the main components, relating to a supernatural power source, seems very unscientific.

The more scientists learn about addiction, the clearer it becomes that chemical solutions will not be available soon. For the foreseeable future, medications will be only an aid to psychosocial treatment. We will still need 12-step self-help groups, behavioural therapies, and exploration of traumatic and everyday experiences that may have disturbed the balance of the reward and inhibition system or the process of learning by association.[31]

Is there a typical type of person who suffers from addiction?

Food addiction or addiction in general doesn't discriminate. People from all walks of life can suffer. Actors and musicians might seem to dominate but that may simply be because they become famous and their troubles are more widely reported. Lawyers, brain surgeons and academics are no more immune to the disease than others.

I once asked a former Broadmoor psychologist (who happened to be running a course at work on dealing with difficult people) whether there was a link between certain mental pathologies and genetically-determined personality type. I wondered if perhaps there might be a preponderance of addicts who lean towards the more people-oriented end of the scale and a greater number of psychopaths from the opposite end. Interestingly she said that there was a link between so-called neurotics and the more people-oriented personality types and that the converse was also true.

Is the path to recovery the same for all food addicts?

Sheppard has found that food addicts fall roughly into five groups in relation to their recovery, or indeed, failure to recover. The first type have had such a horrific time of their addiction that they grab hold of their lifeline of abstinence and become and stay abstinent from the get-go, the second type suffer one relapse and are so horrified with the progression of the disease that they get back on course and maintain long term recovery, the third type suffer years of painful relapse but finally achieve long term abstinence, the fourth try but never manage to maintain long-term recovery and the final group don't want to accept the reality of their disease and never become abstinent.

Chapter 31: Rewiring the Brain

CBT and Rational Emotive Therapy

Sheppard's literature incorporates highly effective and proven tools which are used as standard in psychology today. Essentially, these tools consist of a guided internal dialogue which asks a series of questions to challenge negative thinking by enabling people to identify their feelings, discover their underpinning thoughts and reframe the thoughts in a positive and helpful way. Repeating these positive thoughts as affirmations stops the obsessive thinking and as a result the negative feelings dissipate and stable or even joyful feelings flow in.

Affirmations are just words but words can have an incredibly powerful influence on the brain. Phrased in a negative way words can make us spiral downwards into deeper and deeper depression, phrased in a positive way they can transform our feelings. The power of positive thinking is nothing new of course. And while it does take effort, when practised regularly it becomes second nature. The norm then becomes feeling stable and balanced most of the time with plenty of moments of joy and fewer moments of depression. Who knew that Polly Anna [32] was on to something?

Affirmations work for normal folk too, but usually only a life changing situation or serious health condition will spur people into becoming self-aware and therefore willing to make the effort to change their brain.

God: The baby and the bath water

Humility underpins all of the highly effective 12-step abstinence-based recovery programmes and seeking help from a source more powerful than ourselves is one of the strongest ways of practising humility. The word humility is often associated with being humiliated and being shamed but that's not what's meant in 12-step programmes. The aim is more along the lines of C.S. Lewis's belief that 'Humility is not thinking less of yourself but thinking of yourself less'. It is the obsession with self that makes it so hard for an addict to admit defeat. Yet therein lies the hope—to be able to wave a white flag and ask for help.

Personally, I have found prayer to be incredibly effective and I'm not concerned if ultimately it's a psychological trick or as a result of a flood of dopamine to the brain; the act of praying to an entity greater than ourselves—in my experience and in the experience of hundreds of thousands of other recovering addicts—works. That type of evidence is good enough for me. Prayer seems to be particularly effective when it comes to the strength (not will power) needed to overcome the negative thought patterns that lead a person to use substances. The good thing is you get to choose your own concept of a higher power and don't need to have anything to do with organised religion.

I hear non-addicted people talking of those who relate to a power greater than themselves as ignorant or deluded. Such opinions are a luxury they can afford. For those of us who are addicts and have seen how it has not only saved lives but transformed them, it feels as if it is our critics who belong to the flat earth society rather than us.

Gratitude

Another incredibly effective tool for rewiring the brain is to maintain an attitude of gratitude. The strange thing is that *feeling* grateful is not a requirement, what is required is to think grateful thoughts and repeat grateful affirmations in the mind. If we feel down or negative, forcing ourselves to do an on the spot grateful affirmation has the power to transform our feelings. It has even been shown to increase dopamine levels there and then [33]. Many people would probably rather wallow in self-pity and cynicism but addicts need all the help they can get so this is a good piece of defensive armoury to keep handy.

The importance of getting a sponsor

With the 23 years I spent under an extreme form of spon-
sorship, it might seem strange that I would still advocate en-
listing the daily help of someone experienced with the food
plan and programme of recovery. Quite simply, experience
shows that reporting a food plan every day to a sponsor in-
creases the likelihood of a food addict sticking with the programme.

There are several reasons behind this. Sheppard
points out that with addiction the brain's survival mecha-
nism has gone awry, '...an addict doesn't decide to use chem-
icals, he is compelled to do so[34]' by the brain. Therefore the
mind is flooded with messages that scream 'EAT'. A recovering addict needs to understand that they cannot risk ingesting any trigger foods and that they must accept that
someone experienced in recovery needs to do their thinking
for them while they complete withdrawal. This is because
the survival part of their brain is instinctive and doesn't 'do'
rationality. 'It is never possible for an addict to think their
way out of addiction. No matter how great the intellect, it
can never be used to change the fact that the addiction is
relentlessly operating at the physiological level.'[35]

During withdrawal in particular, thoughts of food will
be fast and furious and it is well known that we move towards our dominant thoughts[36]. An image of donuts comes
to mind, then the taste and feeling is recalled and if not

stopped, it will lead to picking up the food, driven by the instinctual part of the brain. Newcomers to recovery have to start being mindful of these thoughts and a sponsor can help here. The way to keep from picking up trigger foods is to nip the dangerous food thoughts in the bud. If we allow ourselves to obsess over a particular food we will pick it up. If we catch the thought when it first comes to mind, as an unbidden thought, we can counteract it with a rational statement. Addicts need to learn to make use of the cognitive part of their brains, the conscious, rational part to '[...] deal with the failure of the messenger service within the old brain'[37]. A sponsor helps them to build up this atrophied organ. Once through detox, the cravings will subside but obsessive thoughts will continue if they are not swiftly dealt with.

Another reason for working with a sponsor is that, as with prayer, it helps to deflate the dangerous part of the ego—the part that doesn't like to admit failings and weaknesses. Accepting the help from someone more experienced means we aren't trying to use will power (a highly ineffective way to deal with the irrationality of the messages the disease produces in the mind). There's also the accountability to someone else—it's all too easy to want to deviate if we have only ourselves to be honest with.

Committing a daily food plan to a sponsor enables those in recovery to let go of decisions over portion sizes and what to eat for the whole day. The meals for the day are prepared in advance and stored in the fridge or taken as a packed lunch to work. No further decisions need be made other than choosing which utensil to eat it with. It takes away the obsession with what to eat and how much to have, leaving the recovering food addict free to concentrate on life. This freedom from having to decide cannot be underestimated for people who have spent so long obsessing about each and every mouthful of food they've ever eaten. An hour or so is all that's needed to prepare the meals on average for the day. The huge freeing up of mind space that results is an enormous bonus. Many addicts in early recovery are left wondering what to do with all their spare time, a luxury they've never experienced before.

There's also the support and encouragement from someone who has seen it all before and done it all themselves, if not to a greater degree. They know the tricks the mind can play and the measures that need to be taken to prevent a newly recovering addict from succumbing to the dangerous promptings of the psyche. They can, with compassion, point out the faulty thinking that needs addressing if it is a hindrance to recovery.

Sponsors are ready and willing to help voluntarily because they know that in helping others, they can reinforce their own recovery. The constant repetition of the principles of recovery and the attitudes that are adopted provide the necessary reinforcement of their own minds to ensure adherence themselves. Seeing what happens to those who fail to maintain a recovery programme also strengthens the critical, deep-seated acceptance of their own powerlessness over addictive substances. To normal folk, this programme might seem extreme, however, short of being able to manipulate the genetic code of addicts or finding a wonder drug, it seems to be the only effective solution at present.

The 12 Steps[38]

If you haven't come across them before, here are the 12 steps taken and adapted from the original Alcoholics Anonymous programme. The theme of humility is implicit in every step.

1. We admitted we were powerless over sugar, flour, and wheat- that our lives had become unmanageable.

2. Came to believe that a Power greater than ourselves could restore us to sanity.

3. Made a decision to turn our will and our lives over to the care of God as we understood him.

4. Made a searching and fearless inventory of ourselves.

5. Admitted to God, to ourselves, and to another human being the exact nature of our wrongs.

6. Were entirely ready to have God remove all these defects of character.

7. Humbly asked Him to remove our shortcomings.

8. Made a list of all persons we had harmed and became willing to make amends to them all.

9. Made direct amends to such people wherever possible, except when to do so would injure them or others.

10. Continued to take personal inventory and when we were wrong promptly admitted it.

11. Sought through prayer and meditation to improve our conscious contact with God as we understood Him, praying only for knowledge of His will for us and the power to carry that out.

12. Having had a spiritual awakening as the result of these steps, we tried to carry this message to food addicts and to practice these principles in all our affairs.

By swapping the substance of choice, the steps can work for any addiction and have worked for thousands of addicts of all types. The AA Big Book states:

'Here are thousands of men and women, worldly indeed. They flatly declare that since they have come to believe in a Power greater than themselves, to take a certain attitude toward that Power, and to do certain simple things, there has been a revolutionary change in their way of living and thinking. In the face of collapse and despair, in the face of the total failure of their human resources, they found that a new power, peace, happiness, and sense of direction flowed into them' [39]

If you or someone you love needs help, have hope, there is a solution.

Chapter 32: Seeking help

A wealth of information and resources can be found on www.kaysheppard.com and from the suggested reading list that follows. Kay Sheppard also runs a private Facebook group, Breaking Free From Food Addiction, where anyone who wants to learn about food addiction recovery can join, post questions, find answers and find a sponsor to help guide them.

The latest food plan is available on kaysheppard.com as well as the Facebook group page. Other food addiction programs have similar plans but the Kay Sheppard plan has been revised and kept up to date according to the latest research into trigger foods. Each meal consists of weighed or measured portions of starch (such as rice, potato, sweet potato, quinoa, pulses, millet and steel cut oats), protein (fish, white meat and limited red meat and eggs), soy products in moderation, fruit (excluding dried fruit, bananas, mangos, grapes and cherries), vegetables and non-fat dairy products such as skimmed milk, cottage cheese or fromage frais. Healthy oils are also added to the meals after cooking (olive, walnut, avocado and flax are good choices).

Most people are amazed at the portion sizes which seem very large at first (very few are disappointed at the amounts) but they consist of low calorie, high fibre food with all the healthy food groups. Each meal is satisfying and filling and provides the slow burn fuel the body needs until the next meal. Condiments such as mustard, lemon juice, vinegar, herbs, spices and pepper sauces can be used to enhance the meals which hardly need it as they are delicious on their own. Protein can be grilled, poached, oven baked or microwaved. Vegetables can be steamed, boiled or microwaved too.

The food plan needs to be adhered to 100% in order to avoid cravings and to maintain the right balance of carbohydrates and protein for stable brain chemistry. Caffeine and alcohol need to be eliminated completely as these are addictive triggers. Nicotine and any other non-food-based drugs also need to be eliminated for the same reason. It is of course always wise to consult your GP before starting on any regime but most GPs are overwhelmingly supportive of the plan and are often amazed by the results. Many people with type II diabetes and high blood pressure are able to reduce or stop their medication altogether. The plan allows for 45 minutes of moderate exercise every day.

It is important to remember that this is not a diet in the 'slimming' sense of the word. Rather, it is a way of life. Many people who see weight as their only issue treat the food plan as a diet and have good results initially but are rarely able to maintain it. Those who are desperate enough to have reached their rock bottom with the disease of food addiction will be willing to go to any lengths to radically transform their lives. Some have weight to lose to be healthy others do not, but the focus is not on losing weight. Weight loss is simply a healthy side effect of recovery. For these reasons, use of bathroom scales are limited to once a month or discarded altogether to ensure that the focus is on recovery and not weight.

Anyone who has lived as an addict will have many emotional issues to deal with. These issues will raise their ugly heads once the anaesthesia of food or other drugs has worn off. It's therefore necessary to reiterate that a recovery programme is critical in order to sustain abstinence from addictive food. For this to happen, it is essential for addicts who want to recover to understand how to disrupt their faulty reward-response system in their brains so that they can avoid using substances to blot out any stressors. And a stressor can be anything from bereavement to a broken nail. Relapse is very common if a strong programme isn't undertaken. It is believed that between 50 and 90% of all abstaining addicts will relapse in the first year[40].

Starting on the food plan can seem daunting and impossible. This is where the concept of a daily reprieve (well-known in addiction recovery programmes) is helpful. Many addicts live for some far off goal in the future but to maintain recovery, a new mind-set has to be developed. Getting through one day doesn't seem so daunting. The well-worn but never worn-out phrase 'one day at a time' is both comforting and manageable. Soon the days turn into weeks, then months and then years. Recovering addicts can look back with joy as the days of freedom build up. Provided an on-going programme of growth and recovery is maintained there is no reason why the daily reprieve can't be repeated. All of the tools to maintain this recovery can be used: prayer, rational emotive and cognitive behavioural therapy and affirmations, gratitude, a daily inventory, attendance at meetings, giving service and sponsoring others. Yes it's hard work but it's much easier than suffering in the hell of addiction. Recovery 'muscles' are soon built up and the effort feels very minimal after the initial work has been undertaken.

There are plenty of telephone meetings at varying times throughout the week where people from all over the world can dial in to attend, share their experiences and exchange contact details. These can be found in the main food recovery programmes:

www.kaysheppard.com
www.recoveryfromfoodaddiction.org; and
www.foodaddictsanonymous.org).

Many people have no face-to-face meetings in their own locations but successful recovery can be maintained via the phone, email and Skype.

Other Organisations

RFA

www.recoveryfromfoodaddiction.org
Based on Kay's literature and food plan is Recovery from Food Addiction (RFA). RFA is a fellowship of women and men dedicated to physical, spiritual, and emotional recovery by abstaining from sugar, flour, and wheat in all forms and underpinned by the twelve steps of recovery. The goal is 'Recovery from Food Addiction and freedom from the insatiable craving and the merciless obsession of addictive eating'.

There are no weigh-ins or fees. The only requirement for membership is a desire to stop eating sugar, flour, and wheat.

'The food plan and step work lead our members to a new freedom from overeating, compulsive eating, anorexia, and bulimia'.

FA

www.foodaddicts.org

Food Addicts in Recovery Anonymous is an international fellowship of men and women who have experienced difficulties in life as a result of the way they used to eat. Through shared experience and mutual support, help is offered to members who want to recover from the disease of food addiction.

The programme is based on the Twelve Steps and Twelve Traditions of Alcoholics Anonymous. There are no dues, fees, or weigh-ins at FA meetings and membership is open to anyone who wants help with food.

OA

www.avision4you.info

Overeaters Anonymous (OA) offers a program of recovery from compulsive overeating, binge eating and other eating disorders using the Twelve Steps and Twelve Traditions of OA. OA charges no fees; it is self-supporting through member contributions.

OA '...is not just about weight loss, weight gain, maintenance, obesity or diets. It addresses physical, emotional and spiritual well-being. It is not a religious organization and does not promote any particular diet.'

The Maudsley NHS Hospital

http://www.national.slam.nhs.uk/services/adult-services/eatingdisorders/

The Bethlem Royal Hospital, part of the well-known Maudsley Hospital, offers help to patients suffering with anorexia nervosa and other eating disorders. The focus is very much on anorexia nervosa, however, but seems to have had a lot of success in terms of normalising BMI and reducing depression.

Though the Maudsley offers help to people with addiction to drugs, no connection is made between binge eating and food addiction.

Therapy abuse

If you have experienced or are currently in an abusive relationship at the hands of a therapist or health practitioner, TELL (Therapy Exploitation Link Line) is a resource, referral, and networking organization that seeks to help victims and survivors of exploitation by psychotherapists and other healthcare providers 'to find the support and resources they will need to understand what has happened to them, take action, and heal.'

http://www.therapyabuse.org/
E-mail: info@therapyabuse.org

Suggested Reading

Sheppard, Kay. '*Food Addiction: The Body Knows*' Health Communications, Inc., 1993

Sheppard, Kay. '*From the First Bite: A Complete Guide to Recovery from Food Addiction*', Health Communications, Inc., 2000

Sheppard, Kay. '*Food Addiction: Healing Day by Day, Daily Affirmations*', Health Communications, Inc., 2003

Alcoholics Anonymous. New York: Alcoholics Anonymous World Services, 2001, Fourth Edition.

W, Todd, S, Sara, '*Drop the Rock: Removing Character Defects*', Hazelden, 2009

Dwoskin, Hale, '*The Sedona Method*', The Sedona Press, 2009

Grabhorn, Lynn, '*Excuse Me, Your Life Is Waiting. The Power of Positive Feelings*', Hodder, 2011

Postscript

What I didn't mention in my introduction was that there was a third reason for writing this book. I wanted to write it for my parents as well. I wanted to try to help them understand what drove me to act the way I did. Trying to tell them in person seemed so utterly futile. I'm not sure if I've achieved it or if they will ever truly understand how I could have caused them so much hurt, but this is my only way of trying to make amends to them today as well as showing them as much love as I can.

I asked my parents if they would write something that I could include so that they could have their say. My father chose to write down some of what it was like from his perspective. My mother came across some photocopies of letters that she'd sent me when she doubted I was receiving them and so I've included one of them verbatim as it gives a sense of how she was feeling.

From my father:

Eating disorders, like bulimia and anorexia nervosa, are often used by stand-up comedians in their material to extract gales of laughter from their audience. For those who are afflicted by such diseases, it is no laughing matter, nor is it so for the parents or partners of unfortunate sufferers.

Our daughter Candace is one such person who has been to the brink, as it were, but happily after many years battling with the debilitating illness, is now managing her condition with the help of informed counselling. For Candace, she has suffered from the physical pain caused by the illness, the loss of her youth, the break-up of her marriage, and the loss of twenty years of her life during which period she was exploited mercilessly by, in my view, a bogus therapist on the pretext of being 'helped'. This help included the insistence that she should leave her husband, that she cease contact with her parents and that a substantial portion of her take-home pay should be handed over for the purpose of 'helping' other unfortunates. The penalty for disobeying these conditions would result in dire consequences- but I shall leave Candace to expand on the psychological blackmail to which she was subjected.

For her parents, that is her mother Daphne and me, her condition caused us years of extreme anxiety. Throughout her teens her mother went to great lengths to encourage her to 'eat sensibly' but of course at that time during the seventies and eighties these problems were not so widely discussed or publicised as they are today.

When the distressing news came in 1990 that Candace had left her husband after less than two years of marriage and had quit her job without having given any indication that she had felt compelled to take such drastic action, we and her in-laws felt utterly devastated. When we eventually made contact we learned that she had rented a flat in Hackney, north London, (a flat we discovered later to be owned by the 'counsellor') and had taken with her just a few clothes and her two cats. For a while some communication was maintained but as we discovered later, her counsellor insisted that for the sake of his continuing therapy, she should stop.

Despite this interdiction, Candace promised her mother that she would send a note each month. When the note came, my wife would open the envelope and draw out the note with expectations of news only to see that, as usual, it read no more than 'Mum, Am ok. Candace'. She then folded the note and put it back into the envelope, kissed it and placed it with the ever-growing bundle of envelopes. It was a ritual accompanied by sadness and undiminished hope.

Occasionally the note failed to arrive within the agreed month and in the event of no response after sending a letter asking for news, Daphne would travel to Hackney and wait outside the flat in Lewis Road, sometimes for hours (once for four hours), until she could speak to Candace. I still carry the letter she sent to her mother the day after one encounter. It reads:

'Mum. Just to ask you not to wait outside again. It was upsetting and does me a lot of harm.

If you do come again I won't stop to talk but will go straight indoors.

Candace'

It is noted sadly that she doesn't include the words 'Dear' or 'Love' but we had no idea that her counsellor had in fact dictated the letter as she wrote.

However, and it is a big 'however', just over four years ago a dramatic turn of events came about in that on Sunday 7th February 2010 I received an email from Candace: entitled Therapy becoming extreme (see Chapter 26 for the full text).

Can you imagine our reaction to the request from our daughter to 'rent a spare room'?! The plea left us in no doubt that Candace had reached a stage in her relationship with her counsellor that his demands were becoming intolerable. A rescue mission was swiftly organised and the decision was taken by Daphne and me that we should go to Lewis Road that afternoon to collect Candace and, of course, the two cats. Nick, Candace's brother-in-law agreed to come with us. I was pleased to have back-up just in case the 'counsellor' turned up unexpectedly. At that time I had a Ford Ranger truck so that all the essential belongings were quickly loaded up along with the two cats and our dear daughter. Mission accomplished.

Graham Heather 14/04/14

Copy of a confiscated letter from my mother in 1995

Dear Candace,

I do understand that you do not at the moment want any contact but I felt it might be helpful if you could understand a little about my feelings.

On Christmas Eve, I had intended just to hand you the cats' Christmas presents and go, but Daddy really wanted to talk to you as we were both terribly anxious

Therefore, I had not prepared myself for talking and said all the wrong things

It is very difficult to cope with something like this if you have no chance to talk about it. Things have been going on in my head for months, and the crunch came on Christmas Eve (Christmas is always a difficult time emotionally anyway and one thinks about beloved people who cannot be present).

There is a strange thing about motherhood—you cannot stop thinking and worrying about your children, however hard you try and however many times you tell yourself not to.

This may sound exaggerated or emotional, but perhaps it is some biological means whereby to preserve the species or perhaps I'm talking poppycock.

Anyway, the fact of the matter is that I have been deeply unhappy—but that is my problem and I think I have sorted it somewhat, therefore please read on.

I have had very bad feelings about your counsellor, but have come to the conclusion that <u>you</u> know what you need, and if you need to talk to him to 'sort out your head' (as you said) then I <u>must</u> trust you to do what you feel is right.

If this also involves you withdrawing emotionally from the family, then I must trust that you will eventually manage to come back to us.

Reasons for worrying about the situation: - Important – don't forget that we have never met your counsellor and cannot judge his ability.

We have heard very frightening stories about people who have received therapy, and who change completely and will not see their families again.

We have been told that it is not good to become utterly dependent on one counsellor.

You seem to be very much alone, partly because of your job, and we wonder whether it is helpful to have very little contact with other people.

I <u>am</u> sorry about the reference to money to do with your visits etc., but I am sure you realise that when people are worried they often say things which will shock a reaction. I think Dad's mention of Grandpa's money was only that he thought it might result in an acknowledgement, and any communication from you is treasured.

I am trying very hard to come to terms with things and hope you will not stop sending your notes, just to reassure me that you are ok.

Please, I do trust you, but somehow have to let you know how much I love and miss you – as a friend and adviser as well as 'my baby'! Please forgive me, and I hope this does not set back your recovery.

Please could you fill in my questionnaire – we really want to know the answers.

Lots of love

Mutt xxxxxxxxxxX

Questionnaire, please circle your answers

I am well and coping	Yes	No
I passed my last OU exam	Yes	No
I am happy that I passed	Yes	No
I am enrolling on a PGCE course	Yes	No
Ron's abscess is better?	Yes	No
Esme is well and purry	Yes	No
Jake is doing well	Yes	No
I have given homes to 6 other cats	Yes	No
I am keeping reasonably warm	Yes	No
I am careful when walking home on my own from anywhere (see enclosed cutting)	Yes	No
Lily is as cantankerous as ever	Yes	No
I am taking my vitamins etc	Yes	No
Signed _____		

Notes

(a) The Nun's Prayer

Lord, thou knowest better than I know myself that I am growing older and will someday be old. Keep me from the fatal habit of thinking I must say something on every subject and on every occasion. Release me from craving to straighten out everybody's affairs. Make me thoughtful but not moody; helpful but not bossy. With my vast store of wisdom it seems a pity not to use it all, but Thou knowest Lord, that I want a few friends at the end.

Keep my mind free from the recital of endless details; give me wings to get to the point. Seal my lips on my aches and pains. They are increasing and love of rehearsing them is becoming sweeter as the years go by. I dare not ask for grace enough to enjoy the tales of other's pains, but help me to endure them with patience. I dare not ask for improved memory, but for a growing humility and a lessening cocksureness when my memory seems to clash with the memories of others. Teach me the glorious lesson that occasionally I may be mistaken.

Keep me reasonably sweet; I do not want to be a saint-some of them are so hard to live with-but a sour old person is one of the crowning works of the Devil. Give me the ability to see good things in unexpected places and talents in unexpected people. And, give me, O Lord, the grace to tell them so.

Amen.

(Anonymous)

Bibliography

'Eating Disorders 101 Guide: A Summary of Issues, Statistics and Resources. (2002, revised October 2003). The Renfrew Center Foundation for Eating Disorders. Retrieved from http://www.renfrew.org

A Kempis, T. (1400). The Imitation of Christ. Wheaton, IL: Christian Classics Ethereal Library 1998.

ANAD. (2009). Eating Disorders Statistics. Retrieved from http://www.anad.org/get-information/about-eating-disorders/eating-disorders-statistics/

Anonymous, A. (2001). Alcoholics Anonymous (Fourth ed.). A.A. World Services, Inc.

ANRED: Anorexia Nervosa and Related Eating Disorders. (2002). Retrieved from Anorexia Nervosa and Related Eating Disorders, Inc. website: http://www.anred.com/

Doris L. Rapp, M. (n.d.). Sweet Suicide: How Sugar Ruins Your Health. Retrieved January 13, 2015, from YouTube: https://www.youtube.com/watch?v=r8ezchj4wO8

http://www.health.harvard.edu/newsweek/The_addicted_brain.htm. (2002). Retrieved November 23, 2014, from Harvard Health: http://www.health.harvard.edu/newsweek/The_addicted_brain.htm

Korth, R. (2014). My 'Naked' Truth. Retrieved with permission from The Huffington Post.

Maze I, N. E. (2011). The epigenetic landscape of addiction. Ann NY Acad Sci. 2011;1216, 99–113. doi:10.1111/j.1749-6632.2010.05893.x.

Niebuhr, R. (1892–1971). The Serenity Prayer.

Noble, E. P. (2000). *Journal of the Association of European Psychiatrists* 15(2), 79-89.

Patrick F. Sullivan, M. F., Cynthia M. Bulik, P., Jennifer L. Fear, M., & Alison Pickering, B. (1998). *Outcome of Anorexia Nervosa: A Case-Control Study*. Retrieved 2015, from www.psychiatryonline.org: http://psychiatryonline.org/doi/pdf/10.1176/ajp.155.7.939

Sheppard, K. (1993). *Food Addiction: The Body Knows*. Health Communications Inc.

Sheppard, K. (2000). *Food Addiction: Healing Day by Day*. Health Communications Inc.

Sheppard, K. (2000). *From the First Bite: A Complete Guide to Recovery from Food Addiction*. Health Communications Inc.

Silber, T. (2005, September). http://www.ncbi.nlm.nih.gov. Retrieved 2015, from PubMed: http://www.ncbi.nlm.nih.gov/pubmed/16109351

Sullivan, P. F. (1995). *American Journal of Psychiatry*. Vol 152(7), 1073-1074.

Unknown, A. (n.d.). Traditional Scottish Lullaby.

Wang, G.-J. a. (n.d.). Brookhaven National Laboratory. Retrieved from www.bnl.gov: www.bnl.gov/bnlweb/pubaf/pr/2001/bnlpro20101.htm

End Notes

[1] (Traditional Scottish Lullaby)

[2] . (ANAD, 2009).

[3] Luke 9:60, New International Version

[4] Author Unknown, (Attributed to a battle weary C.S.A soldier near the end of the Civil war)

[5] (Alcoholics Anonymous, 2001)

[6] (The Imitation of Christ, 1400)

[7] (The Imitation of Christ, 1400)

[8] (Niebuhr, 1892–1971)

[9] (Food Addiction: The Body Knows, 1993)

[10] (From the First Bite: A Complete Guide to Recovery from Food Addiction, 2000)

[11] (Sheppard, Food Addiction: Healing Day by Day, 2000)

[12] (Sheppard, From the First Bite: A Complete Guide to Recovery from Food Addiction, 2000)

[13] (Sweet Suicide: How Sugar Ruins Your Health)

[14] (My 'Naked' Truth, 2014)

[15] (Food Addiction: The Body Knows, 1993, p. 3)

[16] Breaking Free from Food Addiction — the Kay Sheppard Community (Facebook)

[17] Sheppard, Kay, 27 October 2014 from an article by Kay Sheppard

[18] (Sheppard, From the First Bite: A Complete Guide to Recovery from Food Addiction, 2000, p. 34)

[19] (Sheppard, From the First Bite: A Complete Guide to Recovery from Food Addiction, 2000, p. 34)

[20] (Sheppard, From the First Bite: A Complete Guide to Recovery from Food Addiction, 2000, p. 34)

[21](Noble, 2000, pp. 79-89).

[22] Sheppard, Kay, 27 October 2014, Breaking Free from Food Addiction — The Kay Sheppard Community Facebook Group

[23] Sheppard, Kay, 27 October 2014 (Facebook)

[24] (Wang)

[25] (ANRED: Anorexia Nervosa and Related Eating Disorders, 2002)

[26] (Sullivan, 1995)

[27] ('Eating Disorders 101 Guide: A Summary of Issues, Statistics and Resources, 2002, revised October 2003)

[28] (Sheppard, Food Addiction: The Body Knows, 1993)

[29]

(http://www.health.harvard.edu/newsweek/The_addicted_brain.htm, 2002)

Berke JD, et al. "Addiction, Dopamine, and the Molecular Mechanisms of Memory," Neuron (March 2000): Vol. 25, No. 3, pp. 515–32.

Crabbe JC. "Genetic Contributions to Addiction," Annual Review of Psychology (2002): Vol. 53, pp. 435–62.

Hyman SE. "A 28-Year-Old Man Addicted to Cocaine," Journal of the American Medical Association (Nov. 28, 2001): Vol. 286, No. 20, pp. 2586–94.

Hyman SE. "Why Does the Brain Prefer Opium to Broccoli?" Harvard Review of Psychiatry (May-June 1994): Vol. 2, No. 1, pp. 43–46.

Koob GF, et al. "Neurobiological Mechanisms in the Transition from Drug Use to Drug Dependence," Neuroscience and Biobehavioral Reviews (Jan. 2004): Vol. 27, No. 8, pp. 739–49.

Nestler EJ. "Total Recall – the Memory of Addiction," Science (June 22, 2001): Vol. 292, No. 5525, pp. 2266–67.

[30]

(http://www.health.harvard.edu/newsweek/The_addicted_brain.htm, 2002)

[31]

(http://www.health.harvard.edu/newsweek/The_addicted_brain.htm, 2002).

[32] (Porter, 1913)

[33] Sheppard, K., *Breaking Free rom Food Addiction*, Facebook Group

[34] (Sheppard, Food Addiction: The Body Knows, 1993, p. 47)

[35] Ibid.

[36] Ibid.

[37] Ibid.

[38] (Alcoholics Anonymous, 2001)The Twelve Steps are reprinted with the permission of Alcoholics Anonymous World Services, Inc. Permission to reprint and adapt the Twelve Steps does not mean that A.A. is in any way affiliated with this program. A.A. is a program of recovery from alcoholism only- use of the Steps in connection with programs and activities which are patterned after A.A., but which address other problems, does not imply otherwise.

[39] (Alcoholics Anonymous, 2001)

[40] (ANRED: Anorexia Nervosa and Related Eating Disorders, 2002)

Printed in Great Britain
by Amazon